PRESENTED TO:

_____

PRESENTED BY:

_____

DATE:

_____

Waking Up to Grace: 90 Ways to Start Your Day Knowing You Are Loved
Copyright © 2017 by Jennifer Gerelds
First Edition, October 2017

Published by:

DaySpring

P.O. Box 1010
Siloam Springs, AR 72761
dayspring.com

Bible verses were taken from the following translations:

Quotations marked KJV are taken from the King James Version. Public Domain.

Quotations marked NLT are taken from the *Holy Bible*, New Living Translation, copyright © 1996, 2004, 2015 by Tyndale House Foundation. Used by permission of Tyndale House Publishers Inc., Carol Stream, Illinois 60188. All rights reserved.

Quotations marked CEV are taken from the Contemporary English Version. Copyright © 1995 by American Bible Society.

Quotations marked GNT are taken from the Good News Translation. Copyright © 1992 by the American Bible Society.

Quotations marked NASB are taken from the New American Standard Bible. Copyright © 1960, 1962, 1963, 1968, 1971, 1972, 1973, 1975, 1977, 1995 by The Lockman Foundation, La Habra, CA 90631 90631. All rights reserved.

Quotations marked TLB are taken from The Living Bible. Copyright © 1971 by Tyndale House Foundation. Used by permission of Tyndale House Publishers Inc., Carol Stream, Illinois 60188. All rights reserved.

Quotations marked THE MESSAGE are taken from The Message. Copyright © 1993, 1994, 1995, 1996, 2000, 2001, 2002 by Eugene H. Peterson.

Quotations marked NCV are taken from The Holy Bible, New Century Version®. Copyright © 2005 by Thomas Nelson, Inc.

Quotations marked HCSB are taken from the Holman Christian Standard Bible. Copyright © 1999, 2000, 2002, 2003, 2009 by Holman Bible Publishers, Nashville, Tennessee. All rights reserved.

Quotations marked NRSV are taken from the New Revised Standard Version Bible. Copyright © 1989 the Division of Christian Education of the National Council of the Churches of Christ in the United States of America. Used by permission. All rights reserved.

Quotations marked NKJV are taken from the New King James Version®. Copyright © 1982 by Thomas Nelson. Used by permission. All rights reserved.

Printed in China.

Prime: 70132

ISBN: 978-1-68408-111-0

WAKING UP TO

Grace

90 WAYS TO START *Your* DAY
KNOWING YOU ARE LOVED

JENNIFER GERELDS

TABLE OF CONTENTS

DAWN'S EARLY LIGHT

The LORD's lovingkindnesses indeed never cease, for His compassions never fail. They are new every morning; great is Your faithfulness.

LAMENTATIONS 3:22–23 NASB

The darkness is giving way. Rays of light from a yet-unseen sun have already colored the morning sky with pale pink and glimmers of gold. A new day is literally on the horizon, the sun its herald, inviting you to wake up to experience all that God has planned for you on this day.

But waking up isn't always easy. There are a lot of unknowns that lay outside that bedroom door, and it's tempting not to get out of bed at all. Or if you do, you may simply be going through the motions or getting sucked into everything that seems so urgent in the moment. If you're not careful, the day gets spent (along with your energy), without any real investment being made into what you know matters most.

So how do you greet the sunrise with more intention, hope, and expectation? It begins by waking up to grace—the beautiful reality that your Creator knows you intimately, loves you passionately, and promises to stay with you relentlessly throughout every moment of your life. When you begin each day reflecting on His grace and refreshing your soul with the life-giving power of His Spirit, you can tackle whatever comes your way with a deeper sense of confidence and divine purpose.

Waking Up to Grace is your daily invitation to greet God each morning. May you gain precious insight from each devotional and divine inspiration as you meditate on each scripture. Together may they help you wake up to each new morning with joy and hope, relishing His great love, reveling in His mercies, and receiving the power you need to live each day to its fullest.

It is already the hour
for you to wake up from sleep,
for now our salvation is nearer
than when we first believed.

ROMANS 13:11 HCSB

THE FORECAST
for TODAY

"Come, let us discuss this," says the LORD. *"Though your sins are like scarlet, they will be as white as snow."*

ISAIAH 1:18 HCSB

You heard the weather report, but you weren't sure it would pan out. It wouldn't be the first time you'd awakened in the morning hoping to find snow on the ground, only to see a soggy mess instead. But today was different. The light shining through the cracks in the blinds seemed brighter than before. So you tugged the shade's cord and pulled open the view to a brand-new world. All the dreary browns and grays of winter had vanished; in their place, pristine snow glistened against a brilliant blue sky. Nestled on tree branches, streets, cars, and everything in between, the weather miracle transformed the bleak world you'd known into a scene of magic, mystery, and undeniable beauty.

Better than any forecaster, God has issued a prediction for your day—no matter what the physical weather outside your doors. If you are trusting Him to make the landscape of your life brighter and better than before, you will wake up each day discovering a truth better than transient snow. God wipes your slate perfectly clean each new morning. The failures and regrets of yesterday are completely covered by His love and forgiveness. You are free to enjoy the beauty of all He is as you discover the treasures He has hidden for you in this day.

Unlike the weather, God's miracle of grace never changes, never fades away. You are forever forgiven, simply through faith in Him. Praise God for His mysterious, permanent, and undeniably beautiful gift of daily grace!

Purify me with hyssop, and I will be clean; wash me,
and I will be whiter than snow.

PSALM 51:7 HCSB

HIDE *and* SEEK

He who comes to God must believe that He is, and that He is a rewarder of those who diligently seek Him.

HEBREWS 11:6 NKJV

The stadium is packed, cheers from the crowd roaring. The game has already started, and you know your friend who invited you is somewhere in that sea of faces waiting for you to join him. But the scene seems quite daunting. How will you ever find the one you are looking for in the midst of all those people? Determined, you start scanning, row by row, the faces in the crowd. Up and across, up and across—you search until your eyes lock. This whole time, your friend has been watching you, waiting for you to notice the waves and smile beaming your way that say, "Come up here and join me!"

When you walk out your door this morning, it might seem like just an ordinary day full of responsibilities to fill.

But you have one friend who has invited you to experience it and enjoy it with Him. God is hidden in the details of your day, watching you and waiting to reward you with the pleasure of His presence.

Will He be in the quiet moments you spend studying His Word? In the tender touch of your child's hand? In the conversations you have at school or work? In the car ride to get there? In your thoughts as you consider how to handle this day? The answer is yes! God is hidden in every moment of your life. Seek His face today, and enjoy the reward of His presence with you everywhere you go.

Seek the Lord while He may be found,
Call upon Him while He is near.

ISAIAH 55:6 NKJV

Always

Jesus Christ is the same yesterday, today, and forever.

HEBREWS 13:8 GNT

For a time, people believed the earth was flat. After all, knowledgeable scientists confirmed it, and anyone who could see the horizon could draw a straight line with their finger, tracing the fixed edge of earth against sky. Yep, flat all right. Except that it isn't. And when technology and math advanced far enough ahead, a better perspective emerged. Of course now, with all the outer-space flights and cameras and irrefutable documentation declaring the earth to be round—just like all the other planets—it's hard to imagine we could have ever been that far off.

Life is like that too. We are convinced that something is true or right, and then over time as changes happen, our perspective shifts. In fact, life brings so much change that we can find ourselves desperate for solid ground, some place or truth that stays the same.

He is here, that One you seek—the One who is the same today as He was yesterday and a thousand years before. And He will remain the same forever. As you wake up to face a myriad of uncertainties today, may it calm your soul to remember that God is the solid ground beneath your feet and Jesus is the irrefutable proof of His love for you. His spoken Word and promises are more rooted in reality than the challenges you will face today. Draw near to Him this morning, and thank Him for always loving, protecting, guiding, and forgiving. His faithful friendship is our constant in an ever-changing world.

> *The eternal God of Israel isn't a human being.*
> *He doesn't tell lies or change his mind.*

1 SAMUEL 15:29 CEV

STORM SHELTER

The LORD is like a strong tower, where the righteous can go and be safe.

PROVERBS 18:10 GNT

Though you've slept for hours, you feel like your head just hit the pillow. Already your mind is swirling with thoughts for the day. Of course, there's the usual getting ready, making coffee, facing traffic. But there's more weighing on your mind than the daily grind. That conversation you had with your spouse the other night just didn't sit right, and you're worried you're drifting apart. Your child's project due today is only half finished, and you question your parenting as well as his future. There's a boss to please and laundry to fold, bills to pay and church to attend. You want to do everything well, but you start to feel like you should just hide somewhere and hope everything works out.

Sometimes, escape seems like the most logical

conclusion when faced with the overwhelming circumstances of life. After all, modern psychology tells us we are programmed for either fight or flight when perceived trouble rolls around. Right? The question is: without adequate strength to fight, will you run to the only refuge on this earth with power great enough to protect you and keep you safe forever?

God says His name is a strong tower, and the righteous run to it and find safety. He assures us that no one who comes to Him for protection will be turned away. He is our fortress, our secret place where we can hide, and He Himself will fight the big and small battles we face each day. There is no better place to go today than to the only One with the power to save you in this moment, and your lifetime.

You have been my protection, like a strong tower against my enemies.

PSALM 61:3 NCV

17

GROWING UP

When I was a child, I spoke like a child, I thought like a child, I reasoned like a child. When I became a man, I put aside childish things.

ISAIAH 1:18 HCSB

I f you've ever dropped off your young toddler at a nursery, you've likely seen it happen: unbridled fear and anxiety. Sobs quickly erupt as the little one realizes she can't see her parents. She remains inconsolable until they return and take her back into their arms. Fortunately, as children mature, they gain a greater understanding of their parents' reliability and deep commitment to them, and they walk free of their earlier fears.

The same is true in our relationship with God. Before we really know Him and His character well, we fear that He has already abandoned us or will if we make the wrong

move. It's the mind-set of an infant who doesn't understand the situation. As His beloved children, we are never on the brink of abandonment, despite what our feelings tell us. In fact, even though we feel like God has left and He's out of our sight—especially when we veer off His prescribed path—His sovereign hand is still holding us. Before the world was even created, God devised a plan through faith in His Son that would pave a permanent path back to Him no matter what problem besets us.

We can let the panic, shame, misunderstanding, and fear of our younger years go. We are being held, right in this moment. We have a loving Father, our heavenly Daddy, who has made a way for us to belong to Him forever, and He will never leave us, nor will He forsake us.

> *I pray that you, being rooted and firmly established in love,*
> *may be able to comprehend with all the saints what is*
> *the length and width, height and depth of God's love.*

Ephesians 3:17–18 HCSB

THE RIGHT FIT

The LORD is my shepherd; I have everything I need.

PSALM 23:1 GNT

As you open the door to your closet, you pause. *What should I wear today?* Factoring in the latest trends you've seen at work, school, church, and on social media, you immediately know which options are out. So you search until you find the right ensemble to look presentable and fit in with the people you know will see you today.

It isn't easy to keep up appearances, staying on top of the trends and keeping up a "successful" image. And it isn't just about clothes. It's job performance at work. The parenting or relational prowess at home. For some, it's the size of the house, the type of car, the right neighborhood, or the best school. Whatever it takes to declare to the world, "I have arrived. I've got it together. I, for one, know where I'm going."

But God knows us better. It helps if we just pay attention to Him. He says that people are like sheep—they tend to go in circles when following cues from each other. If we want to know where to go, however, we have to follow the Shepherd.

When you get ready to meet your day today, let your mind look past the pressure of fitting in to following the only One with a real plan for your life. It might not look like everyone else's plan. It might not even seem like a path to success. But in surrender to God's lead, you will find yourself on the right path and in the sweetest of care.

You had wandered away like sheep.
Now you have returned to the one who is your shepherd
and protector.

1 PETER 2:25 CEV

GOOD MORNING, SUNSHINE

For you that honor my name, victory will shine like the sun with healing in its rays.

MALACHI 4:2 CEV

You had hopes of sleeping in this Saturday after a long week at work. The sun isn't even up, though, when you feel the bedsheets ruffle. Soon, you feel two little hands patting your arm. "Lift me up!" your young child whispers in the dark. Trying to stay as asleep as possible, you reach over and pull your little guy up next to you. He snuggles in under the covers, his warm, small body now breathing in sync with your own. As he drifts off to sleep, you have plans to do the same, but suddenly it hits you: this is a sacred moment of amazing grace. Though the sun still hides below the horizon, an even greater light has risen in your heart.

God has created this tiny, living, growing person who trusts, loves, and looks up to you for everything he needs.

He didn't come with a manual, yet you've watched God guide you as a parent who works to meet his every need. In this moment of rest and total trust, you reach to feel his hand. It is small in your own, and you wonder if that's how God feels as He's holding onto you.

Just like you always welcome your child when he comes to you, your heavenly Father will always welcome you anytime you say, "Lift me up!" With delight and affection deeper than that of any earthly parent, He pulls you up into the warmth of His embrace and invites you to rest under the cover of His grace.

He will cover you with his feathers, and under his wings you can hide.

PSALM 91:4 NCV

PIECE *of* CAKE

Taste and see that the LORD is good; blessed is the man who trusts in Him!

PSALM 34:8 NKJV

You're unusually excited this morning. The alarm didn't even have to sound for your eyes to open wide, your feet ready to hit the floor. In your mind, you know it's silly, maybe even a little unhealthy. But you saved the last piece of cake for your morning breakfast, and now nothing stands in your way as you relish the idea of one of life's little indulgences.

Cup of coffee in one hand, fork in the other, the moment does not disappoint. The moist, rich chocolate lights up your taste buds and fills your mind with delight. *God, how can anything be so good?* you wonder, silently giving thanks to the One who created a world with such deliciousness.

There it is: the sweetest truth of all. God, in His incredible kindness, gave us taste buds. Not only did He give us the ability to taste and smell, but He created all kinds of foods with a myriad of flavors to add mystery, variety, and, most of all, pleasure to life. It's just one more evidence that God, our Creator, is good and kind and generous. And it's a reminder that He has invited us to taste and see just how good He is. It's written all through His Word, and it shines all through His world. This morning, enjoy the food and drink God has given you. And let the pleasure drive your thoughts, and your thanks, to the One who made you smile.

Listen carefully to Me, and eat what is good, and let your soul delight itself in abundance.

ISAIAH 55:2 NKJV

GETTING SCHOOLED

My children, we should love people not only with words and talk,
but by our actions and true caring.

1 JOHN 3:18 NCV

Want to know what's really awesome these days? Online school. Yes, you can stay right in your PJs and stumble from your bed to the computer. Class begins when you log yourself in. Before you know it, you've heard a qualified professor explain the topic on your syllabus and gotten your assignment, which you will both research and turn in online.

But even the best online classes require application in the real world. You can't just study for a master's degree in counseling. At some point you have to engage in real person-to-person contact. You can't just get a degree in vet tech. You have to go to a vet clinic and help with real animals. Education without application has no impact in the real world.

The same is true when we learn about God. When the alarm sounds, we're free to roll over and pick up our Bibles and study books to begin our day. It's an incredible necessity and blessing to do so. We can also go online and research topics, hear sermons, and consider the opinions of people across the world. But when God sent Jesus to our world, He showed us what real-life application looks like. It is one thing to think about doing something grand; it's quite another to make it happen. What has God taught you lately through your experiences, studies, or work? This morning, ask Him to show you how to translate His truth into concrete ways to apply your faith.

I will give to the peoples purified lips, that all of them may call on the name of the LORD, to serve Him shoulder to shoulder.

ZEPHANIAH 3:9 NASB

SOUL CARE

*I, the L*ORD*, am your healer.*

EXODUS 15:26 NASB

You can still feel it if you think about it hard enough: the searing pain that shocked your senses the first time you fell off your bike. Knees and elbows scraped down several layers of skin, and the wounds seemed too big to heal. Tears streamed down your face as your mom tried to ease the hurt with bandages. Stiff for a few days, you had difficulty bending in places near the injury, the scabs limiting mobility. But in time, a new patch of pink, shiny skin stretched over the place of past trauma.

It happens so naturally that you might just miss the miracle. God, who made your body, created a system to heal your wounds. You don't even have to understand how it works. Your body just gets busy patching you back together whenever foreign invaders or injuries happen. But what about soul wounds—those injuries to your heart that leave you feeling torn and reeling in pain? The kind that can haunt you the moment you wake up. Aren't those too big to heal? Not in God's care.

The One who created your body to self-heal packs a supernatural power to restore your soul. Just like with your body, it's a process that takes time. Instead of a bandage, you apply the truth of God's love, protection, and provision for you, choosing belief instead of doubt. As you allow God's love to wrap around your hurt, a miracle happens. New life begins to grow where old wounds once were. God seals those places with His grace, healing you by His love and freeing you to face whatever may come your way today.

He restores my soul.

PSALM 23:3 NKJV

Hear my voice in the morning;
at sunrise I offer my prayer
and wait for your answer.

PSALM 5:3 GNT

The GREAT REVEAL

*He reveals things that are deep and secret; he knows what is
hidden in darkness, and he himself is surrounded by light.*

DANIEL 2:22 GNT

You're sitting in your seat, just a few rows back from
the stage. Your eyes are glued to the magician as
he taps on the transparent box before you, urging you to
understand, "There's nothing inside!" To underscore his
point, he drags his arm above, below, beside, and behind
so that you can clearly see there's nothing around the box
except the magician. The fabric drapes down, obscuring
your view for just a second (it shouldn't matter anyway
because you can see all around it), but then whoosh! He
whisks back the cover to reveal something inside the box, a
girl who seems as surprised as you are by the exchange.

Magicians practice countless hours to perfect their
timing and ability to manipulate perceptions. Their goal is

to capture the great reveal. It's impressive, but the magician is only capable of creating an illusion.

Our God, however, is no illusionist. He lets us discover His truth in the same exciting way, but unlike the magician, His great reveals are all they're cracked up to be. He hides the keys to a successful, purpose-filled life in His Word. You keep your eyes focused as you read the same Bible story for the umpteenth time. Then suddenly a new facet of His character or your own looms into view. *How did I not see that before?* you wonder. The secret is God's Spirit. He is the one who reveals what you need to know when you need to know it.

This morning, don't settle for an illusion. Instead, let your eyes fix on the Great Revealer. Ask Him to help you see and understand His direction for your life as you read His Word. Prepare to be amazed!

There is a God in heaven who reveals secrets.

DANIEL 2:28 NKJV

NIGHT LIGHT

I am the light of the world. If you follow me, you won't have to walk in darkness, because you will have the light that leads to life.

JOHN 8:12 NLT

The alarm clock sounds, but your bedroom is pitch dark. You're trying your best not to wake your spouse, who is still sleeping soundly under the covers. Hands outstretched, you feel your way to the dresser, then wall, door frame, doorknob. Then, there it is: the bathroom light switch! Now you can stop fumbling and start a smooth transition into your new day. Of course, if you have to go back for clothes, you use the flashlight on your phone to undertake a stealthy search for all you need, returning to the place where light can shine freely on your day.

Light makes a difference! Whether it's in our morning moments or the darkest nights, our bodies work best when we operate in the light. We're just designed to see better that way. Isn't it incredible, then, that light was the very first thing on God's creation "to-do" list? God spoke and created light before the sun or moon even came into play. How? God's light is different from the kind we see with our physical eyes even though the physical light illustrates the spiritual picture of what God provides.

God tells us in the Bible that He is the Light of the World. The truth we find in Him and what He tells us in His Word sheds the brightest light into the darkest places of our souls. It illuminates where we need to confess and repent, while also lighting our world with all the colors of His grace and forgiveness. God's light ends our fumbling through darkness and sets us free to see His incredible love throughout this day and for the rest of our lives.

God is the LORD, and He has given us light.

PSALM 118:27 NKJV

THIRST QUENCHER

Is anyone thirsty? Come and drink—even if you have no money!
Come, take your choice of wine or milk—it's all free!

ISAIAH 55:1 NLT

You're finally rounding the last stretch of sidewalk before you reach home, your daily exercise nearly complete. Accelerated heart rate, beads of sweat, and panting breath all confirm that today, you got a good workout. But you're parched. Before you head for the shower, you grab a glass from the kitchen and fill it with clean, cool water. As you drink, you instantly feel life and energy returning to your fatigued body. Always hits the spot, you think.

Did you know that more than half of your body is made up of water? It's no wonder you need it, even crave it, throughout your day. But God tells us our souls are no different. He explains the idea in the Bible. Jesus meets a woman at the well where she has gone to draw water. He strikes up a conversation that went like this, "Those who drink the water you draw from this well will get thirsty again, but those who drink the water I give will never be thirsty again. The water I give them will be like a spring welling up inside them giving them eternal life." Then Jesus explains to her that the water He gives is "living water." It's not of this world. It comes from God's own Spirit, filling every child of God.

When God floods our lives with His forgiveness and grace, our thirst for redemption is filled forever. And the invitation to drink from His refreshing and replenishing store of love and hope repeats daily. When you get up this morning, have a satisfying drink of water. As it fills you, let your heart also be filled with the truth of God's everlasting power, forgiveness, and love.

The Scriptures declare that rivers of living water shall flow from the inmost being of anyone who believes in me.

JOHN 7:38 TLB

LOVE LETTERS

What God has planned for people who love him is more than eyes have seen or ears have heard. It has never even entered our minds!

1 CORINTHIANS 2:9 CEV

It's a new day, and you're already hard at work. Your "to-do" list is halfway done, but the pace hasn't slowed and there are miles to go before you sleep. When the workday ends, you head home to face the onslaught of duties that await you. On your way in, though, you stop at the mailbox to get the day's allotment of bills and miscellaneous junk. As you rifle through the contents, though, one small envelope catches your eye. You scan the return address and realize it's from your closest childhood friend, someone you haven't heard from in years! You drop all the other mail on the counter as you plop down in the nearest chair to peruse your new-found treasure. When you're finished, you hold it near your heart. What an encouragement to know you're loved and remembered.

With all the e-mails and text messages today, it's easy to forget the power of a handwritten letter. Unlike all other communications, it speaks of intentionality, value, and time spent crafting it. It is something special.

This morning, there is a treasured communication waiting for you from your best friend. It was written with all the purpose and passion a letter can wield, and it is probably sitting right next to you. God has written about His love and affection for you throughout the Bible—a handwritten letter bearing the history and heart of a God who longs to reconnect with His people. Your God has written you a love letter! Open it—and your heart—to receive it today.

God blesses the one who reads the words of this prophecy to the church, and he blesses all who listen to its message and obey what it says.

REVELATION 1:3 NLT

COMFORTING TRUTH

Praise be to the God and Father of our Lord Jesus Christ, the Father of compassion and the God of all comfort, who comforts us in all our troubles.

2 CORINTHIANS 1:3–4 NIV

It's cold outside, but snuggling deep under the comforter on your bed this morning, you are toasty warm. So at the sound of the alarm, you stick a toe out to assess the likelihood that you will be getting up. *Nope, not gonna happen*, you decide as you pull back your toe. *They call this thing a comforter. Boy, they got that right*, you muse as you snuggle down deeper, shutting out any opportunity for cold to seep in. It just feels too good to be surrounded by warmth and softness to even consider facing the cold, hard reality of the day.

This morning as you revel in the warmth of your bed, let it remind you of another Comforter who envelops you beyond just the morning. God, who walked this earth and experienced the same hard roads of life we all travel, knows all about your worries, your dreams, and your life. Because He knows and is powerful enough to help you, His Spirit in you can comfort you in the very moment you need it most.

Whenever you feel the coldness of this world pressing in on you, wrap your fearful, shelter-seeking heart up tight in the comfort of God's presence. Remember, He not only sees and understands, but He also waits to envelop you in the warmth of His promise never to leave your side. Your God will go with you to comfort and protect you in all you face today and every day. You are able to brave the cold outside, because His love will keep you warm.

The LORD says, "I am the one who comforts you."

ISAIAH 51:12 NCV

The AUTHOR

*All my days were written in Your book and planned before
a single one of them began.*

PSALM 139:16 HCSB

You just wanted to buy an encouraging book for a friend, and maybe pick up a good read for yourself while you're there. But the moment you open the door to your favorite bookstore, your senses are overwhelmed by colors, titles, and topics. It seems like everyone in the world has written something, and it's up to you to search until you find that one selection perfect for the occasion. So you begin the hunt, but you suddenly find yourself engrossed in book after book, the back cover teasers leading you into the stories contained in those pages. Though there is a sea of options, each book has a different and captivating angle on life that broadens your thinking and piques your interest. Each book is an unexpected adventure.

But adventure doesn't just happen in novels. It's happening in and through your life this very moment. Today is not just another day. It's a pivotal page in the story God is writing in and through your life. Today is an integral part of the plot He's weaving to lead you closer to Himself and use you for purposes higher than you can imagine. He is inviting you to trust Him because when you do—when you follow His prompts instead of trying to make your day fit your expectations—the plot thickens, and the threads connect in unpredictably delightful ways.

This morning, hand the pen to God, and ask Him to write His story through your life. With Him in control, you'll know you've made the perfect selection.

Only I can tell you the future before it even happens.
Everything I plan will come to pass,
for I do whatever I wish.

ISAIAH 46:10 NLT

COUNTING *on* JOY

The angel said to them, "Do not be afraid; for see—I am bringing you good news of great joy for all the people.

LUKE 2:10 NRSV

You've spent months planning for this moment, the one where family gathers around the tree for this year's Christmas Day. There is a spark of excitement in the air as the pajama-clad kids file in, hair still tousled from sleep, waiting for the signal to begin. Once videos are rolling, the magic unfolds, and you watch for the one thing you've worked so hard to see: joy. You scan the faces of each person opening their gifts and hope to see happiness over the thoughtfulness, pleasure in the gift, and gratitude for the giver. Surely hugs are in order, yes?

Inevitably, though, the magic comes to an end. People

pack up their gifts and head back to the reality that is life. It's the inevitable valley after pleasure's peak that reminds us real paradise is still lost, at least here on earth. All the money in the world can't purchase lasting peace and joy. But riches from heaven can. God's gift to us is not an object we can open but a relationship we can embrace.

Unwrap and revel today in the grace of God that goes everywhere you do. His grace fills you with infinite joy, blesses your life with every good thing, and promises perfect peace as you trust in Him through every earthly moment. Best of all, God's gift of grace never goes away. Don't settle for temporary treasures. Today, take hold of all God's goodness and celebrate a life lived eternally in His love.

You bestow on him blessings forever;
you make him glad with the joy of your presence.

PSALM 21:6 NRSV

LET FREEDOM RING

He has sent me to proclaim liberty to the captives and recovery of sight to the blind, to set free the oppressed.!

LUKE 4:18 GNT

For twelve years, you went through the paces. Put in the work. Endured the drama—especially in junior high and even some in high school. But at last the day came when all the blood, sweat, tears, and triumphs that were your school experience were completed. Wearing cap and gown, you walked across that stage, accepted your diploma, and walked toward a whole new life of freedom—that place inside your soul that says no matter what lies behind, you have the power to choose where you go from here, and no one can take that away from you.

God tells us that we were born to live in freedom. Every day when you wake up, God hands you the keys to your soul emancipation, the kind that frees you from everything that lies in your yesterdays and gives you a fresh start on your tomorrows. Today is a new day, and you get to choose what you do with this day.

But what about the hurts you carry from the past? Or the ongoing crisis that threatens to remain no matter what you do? Today you have the choice to lay them at God's feet and feel the power of forgiveness and healing. Today you have God's invitation to cast your cares on Him, because He cares for you. You have the choice to entrust your deepest heart cries to His expertise. The key to real freedom is not found in a diploma, job offer, or any life situation. Through repentance, obedience, and trust in God, you are released to stride across the stage of life with all the hope of heaven in your heart and hands.

Where the Spirit of the Lord is present, there is freedom.

2 Corinthians 3:17 GNT

SIGNS *of* SPRING

Behold, I will do a new thing; now it shall spring forth; shall ye not know it? I will even make a way in the wilderness, and rivers in the desert.

ISAIAH 43:19 KJV

Everywhere you look, buds are bursting out on tree branches. The grass is getting greener, the days becoming warmer. Fragrant, colorful flowers fill in the landscape, followed by the larger, spectacular displays in the trees and shrubs. Birds and crickets and frogs and cicadas have come out of hiding and are calling for spring to come. And indeed, spring has sprung. You couldn't be happier. While the snow and stark vestige of winter have a beauty and charm of their own, there's something special about spring and the new hope it brings. The world is just a bit brighter and your breathing lighter, as if with just the change of weather, the weight of the world has lifted a little.

No matter what the season is, let the signs and

reminders of spring grow hope in your heart today. It is no coincidence that the dead of winter gives way to such spectacular growth. God's same goodness grows in you and your life circumstances. Though situations may seem bleak in certain seasons of your life, God's love and purpose never lie dormant. He is affecting the greatest transformation you can imagine, setting the stage for your growth to bloom for His glory.

If you wake up this morning to find yourself in a season of waiting, then set your eyes on God and settle in for the upcoming show. In His time, you'll see, as will we all, the telltale signs of spring. It's then that we will celebrate the growth only God can bring.

Weeping may go on all night, but in the morning there is joy.

PSALM 30:5 TLB

WANTING WISDOM

If any of you needs wisdom, you should ask God for it. He is generous to everyone and will give you wisdom without criticizing you.

Your daughter is at a crossroads. With just a few more months of high school, she's wondering which college? What career? Where should she live? How will she pay for it all? These are just a few of the questions coursing through her mind on a daily basis. But it doesn't end there. She'll need to know where to move once she has her degree. If and who she should marry. Children or no children? Natural or adoption? Be a stay-at-home mom or stay in the workplace? And it seems it's not just the young men and women who are lost for direction. The older we get, the more we come to realize just how many choices come with each new day.

Fortunately, we know Someone who has the answers we

need and the divine perspective we lack. God, who knows the end of the story from the very beginning, sees exactly what is best for our lives. Every ounce of wisdom we need for today can be found in Him and His Word. In fact, God invites us to bring it on. No matter what we've done in the past, God promises not to judge us when we come to Him asking for help. Instead, He pours His wisdom—the divine kind that comes from heaven—into our lives whenever we ask Him to.

Life may throw us a thousand curve balls, but God is the expert on hitting each one out of the park with His eternal perspective and insight. This morning, ask Him to give you the wisdom you need to know and follow His path today

Getting wisdom is the wisest thing you can do!
And whatever else you do, develop good judgment.

PROVERBS 4:7 NLT

I will sing about your strength;

every morning I will sing aloud

of your constant love.

You have been a refuge for me,

a shelter in my time of trouble.

PSALM 59:16 GNT

LET IT RAIN

Let my words fall like rain on tender grass, like gentle showers on young plants.

DEUTERONOMY 32:2 NLT

It starts as an occasional "plunk" on the window pane. Soon, though, the sound shifts to a steady, dull roar not too unlike the sound machine that lulls you to sleep each night. So you climb out of bed and pull back the shades to confirm what your senses have already declared: it's raining. The dark clouds and gentle noise beckon you to climb back in bed for as long as your schedule will allow. It's the perfect moment for a little more rest and maybe some reading. Isn't that why God gave us rainy days?

Maybe. God gives us all kinds of invitations to slow down and rest—not necessarily in bed every time, but to rest in Him and His presence. Just like plants grow hot and tired under the sun's heat, as beautiful and needed as those rays may be, so we dry out and wilt when we fail to slow down and hydrate our souls. God is waiting to pour out His life-giving water into your morning through the nourishing power of prayer and reading His Word. When we take a few moments at the start of each day to soak in His goodness, we are refreshed and empowered to handle the day's tasks in God's strength instead of our own. As we are properly nourished, God produces in us lasting fruit, the kind that blesses and strengthens those He puts around us.

Whether it's rainy or sunny outside your window this morning, take a few minutes before the crazy pace of the day begins. Quiet your soul before God and let the truth of His love pour into and out of your life today.

I lift my hands to you in prayer. I thirst for you
as parched land thirsts for rain.

PSALM 143:6 NLT

BECOMING ONE

My beloved said to me, "Rise up, my love, my fair one, and come away."

SONG OF SONGS 2:10 TLB

He nervously pulls at the bottom of his coat as the bridesmaids slowly file into their places. Then the music changes, and his attention fixes on the place where the one he loves steps into view. His heart seems to stop, and tears begin to flow down his face as he watches his future walk toward him, the life partner and friend God has given him. As she nears, he sees the same look of wonder and joy in her own tear-stained eyes. They are just now beginning to understand the amazing miracle of two becoming one.

Marriage, the way God intended, creates the incredible portrait of intimacy and love every soul longs for. Yet in real life, couples often find that their earthly relationships never fully satisfy their longing or hope for unbreakable connection. Tempers flare, communication crumbles, and the tyranny of life in a broken world takes over. They find themselves struggling to preserve their lifelong commitment.

Yet where our earthly relationships may fall short, our faithful God never does. Calling us His Bride, God invites us into a permanent love commitment that knows no bounds. He leads us to a place where we are free to let down our guard and revel in His delight over us. Whether you are married or not, you have a Husband who pursues, cares for, protects, and cherishes you like no other. It is out of this love God has first given to us that we learn how to love one another.

Draw close to your first love this morning, and marvel at the magnitude of God's amazing grace. Invite His Spirit to strengthen your earthly relationships as He pours His love into and through you.

I have loved you with an everlasting love;
therefore I have continued my faithfulness to you.

JEREMIAH 31:3 NRSV

HUES *of* HOPE

He woke up and rebuked the wind, and said to the sea, "Peace!
Be still!" Then the wind ceased, and there was a dead calm.

MARK 4:39 NRSV

The storm's severity caught you off-guard. Though you could see the dark clouds looming ahead as you drove across town, you had no idea how fast and hard the rain could fall. So you pulled off to the side of the road, deciding to wait it out. As suddenly as it started, it stopped. The clouds pushed past, and the sun came streaming down through crystal-blue skies. But before you could start back out on the road, curiosity caused you to turn and look. There it was! A rainbow was shining brighter than the sun's rays on rain-soaked streets, painting the dark sky behind with an amazing palette of color.

Is it any wonder that God chose a rainbow to promise hope to Noah and his family after such a horrific flood?

Rainbows are God's colorful reminders that there is no storm in our lives too strong or too dark that God can't create something beautiful out of it.

As you wake up today, what storms—if any—loom on the horizon? Even if one takes you by surprise, you do not need to be afraid. Just as Jesus stilled the waves and calmed the storms for His disciples, so God has the power to carry you through whatever the day brings. The light of His presence packs a remarkable power to shine through our moments and reveal a beauty we never thought possible. Storms are simply our invitation to trust Him as He works miracles into every moment.

> *When … the rainbow appears in the cloud,*
> *I'll see it and remember the eternal covenant*
> *between God and everything living …*
> *every last living creature on Earth.*

GENESIS 9:16 THE MESSAGE

Coloring Love

God looked over everything he had made; it was so good, so very good!

GENESIS 1:31 THE MESSAGE

D o you remember the first time you opened a box of crayons? The smell of wax and paper tightly wrapped around each beautiful color arrested your senses and set your imagination to flight. In an instant you were an artist, transforming the ordinary white sheet of paper before you into lines and shapes and patterns that rendered your inner world awash with color right before your eyes. What were stick figures and circular flowers to older, less-sensitive souls were your early masterpieces, your version of Eden.

But what if instead of a full spectrum of differing hues, your box had only one color? It may have entertained you for a moment but certainly wouldn't have held your attention.

There's beauty in diversity and pleasure in harmony. We witness the same miracle every time we open our eyes and really see the world around us. God did not make our world a monochromatic experience. Brilliant color fills the skies, the trees, and the land. Eyes and skin and cars and houses and flowers and oceans all treat our eyes to a feast of festive colors that turn the entire world into an extraordinary work of art.

As you rise and shine this morning, recapture the wonder of color as you get ready for the day. Notice the hues in everything your hands touch and all your eyes see. Then give thanks to the One who prized you enough to color your world with His creativity and love, making your brilliant, beautiful life into an integral part of His magnificent masterpiece.

Oh yes—God takes pleasure in your pleasure!
Dress festively every morning.
Don't skimp on colors and scarves.

ECCLESIASTES 9:7 THE MESSAGE

KEYS *to* FREEDOM

Forgive us for our sins, because we forgive everyone who has done wrong to us.

LUKE 11:4 NCV

Your mind keeps wandering back to the person you trusted—the one who turned on you. Your stomach tightens. Though the trespass happened long ago, the wound feels fresh. You may deny it, stuff it, and do your best to push it away, but experience warns you to build up walls around your heart to protect it from future pain. Relationships just aren't worth the risk, your wary and weary heart concludes. And so the chains that bind you to the past and keep you from feeling the full pleasure of today grow ever tighter. You need a different kind of Savior.

Thank God you have one who knows your hurts and

cares deeply about the wounds in your soul. He invites you to come close and washes you clean. He tends to your heart with whispers of true and lasting love. Drawing near, light floods the darkness, and you can see the key to freedom dangling in front of you. But to use it will change the course of your life forever. Freedom happens through forgiveness—God forgiving you, and you forgiving those who have hurt you. Forgiveness doesn't mean condoning the offense. Instead it means setting yourself free. In miraculous exchange, as we set the captives of our anger and bitterness free, our hearts break forth in glorious freedom.

This morning, take a moment to ask God to search your heart for any traces of bitterness that are still holding you captive. As He reveals your soul's secret wounds, pray that God will heal those places with His love and empower you to forgive on your path to freedom.

Whoever has a complaint against anyone;
just as the Lord forgave you, so also should you..

COLOSSIANS 3:13 NASB

PUPPY LOVE

You will show me the path of life; in Your presence is fullness of joy; at Your right hand are pleasures forevermore

PSALM 16:11 NKJV

You are sitting at your computer desk, trying to make heads or tails of the stack of bills lying beside your keyboard. "How on earth did we spend that much money eating out?" You ponder aloud as you stare at your online checking account. Already, you can feel the throb of stress starting to build in the front region of your head.

Then you hear the bark. Not a mean one, just a questioning little yip from your small but ever-so-loyal dog sitting at your feet looking up at you and begging to be in your lap. So you acquiesce, reaching down to pull up the soft, furry ball of love. Licking on arms and hands immediately commences, but eventually he settles in for a nap, sleeping soundly without a care in the world. As you stroke the soft fur between your fingers, you can't help but smile. Without a word, this small creature—by his mere presence—has eased away some of life's load. And you wonder, *Is this why God made pets?*

Truth is, pets are just one of the delightful ways God shows His love and concern for us. He didn't have to give us dogs with soft fur and tender tongues, cats that purr when petted, and a host of other domesticated creatures people welcome into their homes. God intended animals not only to showcase His creativity and power but also to give us pleasure. As you love on your furry family member this morning, thank God for His soft reminders that He always has your best interests at heart.

GOD's not finished.
He's waiting around to be gracious to you.
He's gathering strength to show mercy to you.

ISAIAH 30:18 THE MESSAGE

GOOD NIGHT KISSES

At day's end I'm ready for sound sleep, for you, GOD, have put my life back together.

PSALM 4:8 THE MESSAGE

Your phone's alarm sounds through the darkness of your bedroom. As you fumble to find it and shut off the most unwelcome noise, you sleepily consider possible options for delaying the day. You could call in sick, you think for a moment. No, lying's no good. But then the thought, *Just hit snooze!* But in the blink of an eye, the alarm is sounding again.

The struggle is real, and getting up seems unavoidable. Then it hits you—it's Saturday! You can sleep in! The hectic pace of your regular week can wait for another day. Today you can rest and savor the simple pleasure of extra sleep. So you put your phone on airplane mode and settle back in for a long, relaxing morning.

Sleep—the good, sound, rejuvenating kind—is a sweet kiss from our heavenly Father. It's comforting to know that He doesn't make the same driving demands we find virtually everywhere else. No, our God invites us to rest, and often. He encourages us to rest from our attempts to earn His favor, because we already have it. Rest from the need to control our lives and those around us, because He is the only one with that kind of power and has promised to work everything out for our good. Rest from the maddening pursuit of pleasing everyone else. He simply offers Himself as a quiet place for us to lay down our burdens and relax in His care. When we take Him up on the offer, our souls rejuvenate. Having rested in His love, we are ready for that alarm in the morning and all the adventure that awaits.

Come to Me, all who are weary and heavy-laden,
and I will give you rest.

MATTHEW 11:28 NASB

SUNRISE SURPRISE

His coming is as certain as the morning sun; he will refresh
us like rain renewing the earth in the springtime.

HOSEA 6:3 CEV

It is still, quiet, and dark outside. In the wee hours of
the cool summer morning, you wrap yourself in your
warmest robe and venture into the dark, just far enough to
find your favorite outdoor chair. Wiping off the dew, you sit
and wait. Slowly, your eyes adjust to the darkness, but the
trees and shrubs nearby seem whitewashed silhouettes in a
lonely, gray world.

Then it happens. The first rays of light peek over
the horizon. Sky and hills, branches and blades of grass
catch the energy, and color pours out onto every lighted
surface. Like magic, light dispels the darkness, and animals
respond on cue, chattering and chirping, their call to greet
the morning. As pink and orange hues paint the pale blue

sky, you soak up the beauty, the miracle of this morning's sunrise. And your heart joins in their song, the celebration of the sunrise's Creator.

If you rise early enough each day, you will see this blessing again and again. Each day God brings our earth back around for the sun to shine on our lives once more, initiating beauty from the very beginning. It begs us to begin our day mindful of a Master Painter, Sustainer, and the source of all we call beautiful. Our hearts burst with praise and worship for the only One who can transform darkness into a magnificent, light-filled world of future promise. He is here in this sacred moment. Here where light chases away the darkness. Here where He reminds us day after day that His goodness rises to greet us and the sweetness of His morning touch lingers for the rest of our day.

The heavens are telling of the glory of God;
and the expanse [of heaven] is declaring the work of His hands.

PSALM 19:1 AMP

CONNECTION

Let us have confidence, then, and approach God's throne, where there is grace. There we will receive mercy and find grace to help us just when we need it.

HEBREWS 4:16 GNT

Not that long ago, cell phones didn't exist. Land lines were tethered by stretchy, spiraling cords that kept communication limited to the places where the cords could reach. If you were stuck in traffic and needed to tell your appointment how late you'd be, you simply had to make your excuse in person once you finally arrived. There was no such thing as checking e-mail or social media or surfing the Internet to make purchases, locate maps, or look up menu choices.

But today, communication is virtually instant all the way across the world. Technology has bridged the gap that existed between people in different places throughout the ages. When you stop to think about it, the cell phones in

everyone's hands may be annoying at times, but they're also a communication miracle.

But an even greater miracle than cell phones has happened. And that miracle took place long before telephone lines were even a developing thought. When Jesus paid for our sins on the cross, He reconnected the lines of communication between us and God. His provision paved the way for instant access to the Father anytime, anywhere we are. Whether we choose to talk out loud or pray in our minds, God hears every word we say. And He answers, sometimes even while we're speaking—the connection is that strong.

This morning, before you pick up your phone to check the latest everything, make that most important connection with God. Commit your day, your words, and your life to Him. And thank God that His reception works wonderfully everywhere you go.

We have also obtained access through Him by faith into this grace in which we stand, and we rejoice in the hope of the glory of God.

ROMANS 5:2 HCSB

MORNING SONG

Sing to the LORD a new song; Sing to the LORD, all the earth.

PSALM 96:1 NASB

If you are still, you will see it. And if you listen, you can hear a symphony playing right outside your door. Don't bother looking for a bassoon or clarinet, a cello or a trumpet. No man-made instruments are needed in God's performance hall. Instead, living creatures contribute their sound of praise to the Creator, with pitch and rhythm unique to their kind. Tree frogs chirp from secret hiding places. Bullfrogs bellow in low, steady calls. Cicadas and crickets sound like maracas, and birds are the woodwinds, their melodies sweetening the sound.

Are you delighted by the free concert outside your door, day after day? God certainly is! He created all of His creatures to declare His praise in ways only they can.

Something about music soothes our souls. It reminds us of a beauty greater, a power stronger, and a purpose eternal that exists beyond ourselves. Music, in all its forms, can lead us to worship when we remember the One who put the song in our hearts in the first place. Perhaps that's why God chooses to live in the praises of His people. When we join in with all of creation, singing God's praise from grateful and thankful hearts, our lives join creation's symphony of praise, and we are music to God's ears.

Whether you put on a praise CD, play worship music from your computer, or simply sing in your heart to God this morning, let this day begin with a heart that stands in awe of His beauty and love. Let His greatness inspire your heart and lips to declare His praise today.

It is good to sing praises to our God;
for it is pleasant and praise is becoming.

PSALM 147:1 NASB

Satisfy us each morning
with your unfailing love,
so we may sing for joy
to the end of our lives.

PSALM 90:14 NLT

COMING HOME

God is not ashamed for them to call him their God, because he has prepared a city for them.

HEBREWS 11:16 GNT

Your children are grown, each working hard to make their own way in the world. And you are proud. Thankful. Always eager to answer the phone whenever one calls with a need. Though the day-to-day labor of raising children has ceased, your love and prayers certainly have not.

So when the holidays roll around and your children announce that they all will be coming home this year to celebrate with you, your heart stretches wide with the same giddiness you remembered from Christmases long ago. The music, the laughter, crackling fires, and fragrance of pine and cinnamon add to the festivities, but you know you don't need a gift under the tree. There is nothing more precious to you than the presence of your family. It is the present. You thank God for the blessing that they are all coming home.

Coming home. It's the heart call inside every one of God's kids. Every reunion, each Christmas or Thanksgiving gathering is simply a foretaste of the moment we finally reach that permanent place where joy and love and peace never cease. That place where we know we are safe, richly blessed, and bound together to celebrate God's great love forever.

This morning, thank God for your home and family here on earth and the wonderful times you have when all of you are under one roof. Then celebrate with God in advance for your future home with Him and all of His huge family!

Happy are those who are strong in the Lord,
who want above all else to follow your steps.

PSALM 84:5 TLB

ROOTS

Keep your roots deep in him, build your lives on him, and become stronger in your faith.

COLOSSIANS 2:7 GNT

There it is, sticking up like a stealthy intruder right in the middle of your garden bed. You walk over and bend down to pull up the errant oak tree seedling that has sprouted in the middle of your tomatoes. But much to your surprise, the short seedling seems to have hidden strength. So you wedge the weight of your body against the tree's resistance, and slowly you feel its root system give way. With the sound of a garment being torn, the roots break and release their grip in the ground, with long tendrils of underground anchorage slipping to the surface. Once fully uprooted, the small seedling looks several feet in length. How could so much be happening underground with so little to show up top? you wonder.

It's funny how the small things can have that kind of impact in our lives. A little negative comment here, a white lie there, can suddenly take root in our souls. Left unchecked, bitterness and apathy spread out with tenacious tendrils, burrowing deeper into our hearts and minds, choking out the love and life that once dominated. On the surface, others may only see a small discontent. But inside, anger has taken hold with a vicelike grip. To uproot it requires the full weight of your entire person, leaning in the opposite direction, with reliance upon God's great mercy. But once it's removed, the seeds of God's love and forgiveness are freed to grow and bear the kind of fruit you want to see in your life.

This morning, ask God to uproot any bitterness, complacency, or dishonesty lurking in your soul. Ask Him to plant in their place a harvest of love, joy, and peace.

May your roots go down deep
into the soil of God's marvelous love.

EPHESIANS 3:17 TLB

WINDS *of* CHANGE

Just as you can hear the wind but can't tell where it comes from or where it will go next, so it is with the Spirit.

JOHN 3:8 TLB

It's summer, and the stagnant heat of the day is taking its toll on your tired body. You stop walking and lean forward with locked arms braced against your knees as you try to catch your breath. *Why did I think it would be a good idea to go hiking in the woods today?* you wonder. Truth be told, you thought the trees' shade would be adequate cover to keep you cool. But you hadn't factored in how stifling heat can be without any breeze to cool you off. Then suddenly, as if on cue, the rushing of a cool, refreshing wind blows through the trees, bending their branches and bathing you in a literal breath of fresh air. Smiling at God's invisible refreshment, you find the strength to finish your course.

Isn't it amazing how something we can't even see can have the power to bend (and at times, even topple) tall trees and lower our temperature? We may not even understand where the wind came from, but we enjoy the benefits and marvel at its power. God says His Holy Spirit moves in the same way. We can't see Him with our eyes, and we don't understand fully how He does it, but He blows into our lives, refreshing our dry and weary souls and filling us with the supernatural power we need to keep walking with God.

If you woke up this morning in need of refreshment from the sapping, dry heat that life often brings, ask God to cause His blessed wind to blow into your soul. His soothing love can cool your frustration and fill you with energy.

Awake, north wind. Come, south wind.
Blow on my garden, and let its sweet smells flow out.

SONG OF SOLOMON 4:16 NCV

DIVE IN

Trust the LORD with all your heart, and don't depend on your own understanding. Remember the LORD in all you do, and he will give you success.

PROVERBS 3:5–6 NCV

I'm too old for this, you think as you fidget with your vest. *Planes are meant for flying, not jumping out of.* Your thoughts quickly escalate, as does the churning in your stomach. Then it's time. Your much-more-experienced partner attaches himself to you, covering your back and ushering you toward that gaping opening in the plane. Before you even have time to think, though, you are free-falling, wind rushing up as your body plummets down. Utter terror combines with excitement, all of it heightened by the stunning beauty of the world below you and an entirely new vantage point. As the parachute deploys, the wonder of it all sinks in. Life seems different now that you have experienced a beauty you had never known before. Grateful for the ground and the thrill of a lifetime, you vow never to forget the moments you soared above it all.

For many of us, skydiving seems like a reckless or pointless endeavor. But those whose lives have been changed by it understand the attraction. Something sacred and sensational happens when you jump into the unknown, trusting that you will be held as you enjoy the ride.

Today, as you get up to face what lies ahead, realize that you aren't alone. Your much-more-experienced partner—God—has got your back covered, and His powerful presence is tethered tightly to your life. If He leads you into unexpected places, embrace the adventure and let your fears settle in the knowledge that He has everything under His control. See the world from His vantage point, and marvel at the beauty of a life lived trusting in Him.

This is my command—be strong and courageous!
Do not be afraid or discouraged.
For the LORD your God is with you wherever you go.

JOSHUA 1:9 NLT

The PURSUIT

Nothing can ever separate us from his love. Death can't, and life can't. The angels won't, and all the powers of hell itself cannot keep God's love away.

ROMANS 8:38 TLB

What is it about romance movies that keep us coming back for more? Each one is simply a story about two people, but the intrigue of connection and the mystery of how it happens arrests our hearts, minds, and souls every time. We sit riveted, waiting to catch the flicker in his eyes and the lingering look into hers as they pass each other in the crowded marketplace. We worry uncomfortably as twists and turns seem to throw them off course for the love we hope they're destined for. And of course, when the obstacles fade and they at last embrace, a rush of hope and excitement fills our hearts even though we know it's just a movie. The beauty of pursuit, of being discovered, loved, and held, satisfies—if only for a moment—that deep soul desire we feel in real life.

But romance isn't just a Hollywood fabrication. You have a lover, a pursuer, a soul mate who desires to lavish you with love. To look at you in utter delight and declare your beauty and infinite worth. To embrace you with a love that will never let you go.

The twist is that it isn't your earthly partner. God, the Author of romance, is the only one who loves us in this pure and noble way. He left everything He had in heaven just to make you His own. He loves you in spite of your flaws, transforming you into a treasure of true beauty. His is a love story like no other, ending with an actual "happy ever after."

Will you come to rest in the warmth of His embrace? Choose, this morning, how you want to see the story end and watch how real passion begins.

The Son of man is come to seek and to save that which was lost.

LUKE 19:10 KJV

SHINE ON

Don't hide your light! Let it shine for all; let your good deeds glow for all to see, so that they will praise your heavenly Father.

MATTHEW 5:16 TLB

You're hungry, and even though you've been trying to stay away from fast food, the tyranny of the day takes over and you steer into the drive-thru and place your order. As you pull up to the window, you fumble for some cash or a card to cover the small expense. And then you get the news. "It's okay, you're paid up," the cashier says, smiling. "The person ahead of you in line paid for your meal." "What?" you ask, incredulous that someone who doesn't even know you would be so kind.

As the impact of this simple gesture sinks in, you drive to the next window and pick up your food. Suddenly, the rushing, hectic pace of this demand-driven day comes to a halt. Unexpected love and favor have altered the scene, giving you a taste of something far better than the hamburger you hold in your hands. It's the savory sensation of being noticed, and being loved for no other reason than the one who blessed you simply chose to do so.

Random acts of kindness get our attention because they so rarely happen in a me-centered world. They are like rays of light breaking through a darkness that shrouds the world we live in. As God's child, you possess that life-changing light inside you. When you notice others' needs and take action to meet them, your life is like a star shining out in a dark universe. How will you let God's light shine through you today?

*Those who put others on the right path to life
will glow like stars forever.*

DANIEL 12:3 THE MESSAGE

DRINK UP

*I am calm and quiet, like a baby with its mother. I am at peace,
like a baby with its mother.*

In the middle of church, you can hear the discontent
build. Piercing people's quiet concentration, a baby starts
to fuss, with short groans and grunts of discomfort. You
hear the nervous mother rustling for pacifiers, whispering
words of comfort to her little one. But he will not have
it! Soon the short cries stretch into all out shrieks of what
sounds like intense agony. Heads start to turn as the young
mom works her way quickly up the aisle, baby siren blaring
in her arms. Only one thing can satisfy his tiny little soul,
and she knows it—her body is already responding to the
sound, readying itself for the feeding. And so she does,
in the quiet of the nursing room. Holding him tightly to

herself, her own life supplies the nourishment that his body demands. Once he's satisfied and content, she slips back up the aisle and into her seat.

Babies are often our greatest teachers. In them, we see our own helplessness, our basest needs demanding satisfaction. How beautiful that God would create such a portrait of how He meets those needs. How He holds us close and pours out His own life into ours so that we can be fed and filled. Because of His love and care, we grow up into the people we were created to be.

Is your soul unsettled this morning? Do you find yourself irritable or restless, unable to find anything on earth that can pacify your needs? Turn to the Source of life, hope, and love, and drink your fill from the God who cares for you. He will hold you close this day and every day.

The humble will eat and be satisfied;
those who seek the LORD will praise Him.

PSALM 22:26 HCSB

IT IS FINISHED

I am sure that God, who began this good work in you, will carry it on until it is finished on the Day of Christ Jesus.

For weeks, months even, you have labored for this moment. It began with an idea, an inspiration to create a work of art you hoped would fill that space in your home perfectly. Then you shopped in stores and online, searching for the right tools and materials to make your vision come to life. Over time, piece connected to piece, and your idea became reality. Now, at long last, your creation is complete, ready to take its place on the wall you reserved for it. Standing back, you smile in deepest satisfaction. The finished piece is your reward, confirming your efforts were worth it all.

Finishing tasks, even the smallest ones like vacuuming a room or loading the dishwasher, brings a level of satisfaction. It's a reclaiming of order, if only for a moment, a restorative accomplishment in the middle of mundane details. But the projects that take longer, even lifetimes to complete, bring the greatest reward of all. These are the achievements worth standing ovations, the prize yielding the most glory.

You, child of God, are a great work of art in process. Before you were born, He planned exactly where He would place you in this world, unfolding beauty and boldness like only you can. If you wake up this morning frustrated by your failures, remember that your life is not yet complete. The Master Designer is strategically crafting every moment of your life, shaping your character into one that matches the perfection in His mind. So do not worry. He has promised to finish the work He has begun, yielding His glory through you all along the way. Your task today is to surrender to His plan as He finishes His perfect work in you.

We are his workmanship, created in Christ Jesus unto good works.

EPHESIANS 2:10 KJV

POWER SOURCE

We now have this light shining in our hearts. ... This makes it clear that our great power is from God, not from ourselves.

2 CORINTHIANS 4:7 NLT

You tested the lights before you began stringing the tree. You even purchased new ones to ensure the greatest quality and success. It took an hour of struggle, but you wound them in place so that tiny white lights could brighten up every branch. So why aren't they all working? you wonder, moaning as you retrace the wires. You stare dumbfounded at the one, rebellious strand that refuses to light. Finally, you find it! As you tugged around the tree, one of the plugs had pulled away from its power source. You smile as you quickly reconnect the cords. Voila!

Some things just require connection to function. We are like that. We need love and support from other people, kind of like all the other lights on our life strand. But without a power source, we can't shine. Without an outside energy surging through our souls, we end up strung out without a purpose. God tells us, though, that He made us with the purpose to shine for Him. We make the world a more beautiful place when we're living as we were designed.

But when we stand back and take a look at our lives, do we see vibrant light pouring out or sparsely lit bulbs due to the strain and pull of our daily lives? If we want to live with power, we have to check our Source. Are we connected in heart, mind, and soul to the One who made us? Are we relying on Him to fill us with His supernatural energy, or are we trying to wind through life on our own? This morning, take time to reconnect with God, who alone can give you the charge you need to shine brightly for this new day.

I am the vine, ye are the branches:
He that abideth in me, and I in him,
the same bringeth forth much fruit.

JOHN 15:5 KJV

The VERDICT

Through Christ Jesus the law of the Spirit who gives life has set you free from the law of sin and death.

ROMANS 8:2 NIV

The media has been abuzz for weeks following what appears to be a cut-and-dried case. The defendant was caught red-handed in the middle of an unspeakable crime. Everyone who heard about it was outraged at the evil. And everyone waited on the edge of their seats, eyes glued to the TV as the jury read the verdict. "Not Guilty!" the jury foreman declared. A pause of unbelief. Then the uproar. Cries of anger and disbelief poured out from every corner of the courtroom, except the one where the defendant stood speechless, marveling at the mercy verdict.

Our desire to see justice prevail comes from our Father's heart, who tirelessly defends the downtrodden. But from the same heart flow rivers of mercy for tired souls destined for destruction without His saving grace. In every sense, we are all criminals caught in acts of egregious sin against a Holy God. But our cases are not lost because we have a representative who pleads for us. Better still, He paid the price for the life-debt we owed. Miracle of all miracles, we as former prisoners to sin now walk free as the prized and beloved children of God, no matter how much murmuring you hear from the crowd or even your own mind. Your case has been tried and the verdict is in. You have been found not guilty, cleared of all guilt by the only begotten Son of God.

As you rise to freely enjoy the day, remember that your freedom came at the highest cost to God. May His unmerited mercy on your behalf fill you with the assurance of His love and the determination to show that love to all, including those who deserve it the least.

The wages of sin is death, but the gift of God
is eternal life in Christ Jesus our Lord.

ROMANS 6:23 HCSB

It is good to proclaim
your unfailing love in the morning,
your faithfulness in the evening.

PSALM 92:2 NLT

STRONG BREW

*You prepare a table before me in the presence of my enemies; ...
my cup overflows.*

PSALM 23:5 HCSB

It's early in the morning, and you know the routine. Climbing out of bed, you make your way to the coffee pot. Rinse. Fill. Pour. Liner in. Spout turned. Lid closed. Push the button. Wait for the magic to happen. Actually, you rarely sit and wait for the coffee pot to fill because you're busy making the breakfast to go with your brew. And slowly, drop by drop, the pot fills up until it's ready—you're ready—to grab your favorite mug and sit down for a few sacred moments before the din of the day takes over.

It's funny how something as simple as a coffee pot, simply doing its job, can give us a life lesson along with a jolt of caffeine. It reminds us that whatever we put into our relationship with God determines what comes out and how strong it is in our lives. But just like that pot of coffee, a full and rich relationship with God doesn't happen instantly. It builds, one moment at a time, each time you choose to talk to Him in prayer, read what's on His heart from His Word, listen to and sing songs of worship, spend your time wisely, and view every part of life as under His control. Every thought you think and moment you spend is another drop, either filling you with more of Him or more of whatever it is you're choosing over Him.

This morning, choose to fill up on the joy of God's presence. Ask Him to pour out His Spirit on your day, and help you to live every moment in His grace. And enjoy your coffee!

May the God of hope fill you with all joy and peace
as you believe in Him so that you may overflow
with hope by the power of the Holy Spirit.

ROMANS 15:13 HCSB

FALLING UP

The LORD will hold your hand, and if you stumble, you still won't fall.

PSALM 37:24 CEV

Arm upstretched, she slipped her tiny hand into the strong grip of her daddy's as they began walking together down the sidewalk. His every stride confident and sure, her small legs working hard to match his pace. The world around her shined bright, beautiful, and full of intrigue. Suddenly, just as her eye caught a jogger headed their direction, her foot slipped off the edge of the sidewalk. The bend of her ankle buckled her knee and she felt the weight of her body start to give way.

But she didn't fall. Instead, her father's grip grew tighter, the strength of all he was held her, even lifted her, suspended for a few seconds in air. Dangling there by her father's brute strength, she knew what it was to be held.

Loved. Protected. And the two continued walking on their way.

Just like that little child, you have an opportunity to reach up to your heavenly Daddy this morning and put your hand in His. You are His pride and joy, the apple of His eye. He will keep you close beside Him as you go about your day. Linked to your Creator, you are free to explore all that this day has to offer without fear. Be bold in your witness. Curious in your study. Generous in your giving. Risk the adventure of walking with God with a heart wide open. It's not that you won't ever trip up. It's that when you do, God will hold you up with His mighty right hand.

Because you are sons, God has sent the Spirit of His Son into our hearts, crying, "Abba, Father!"

GALATIANS 4:6 HCSB

PARTY TIME

They shall celebrate the fame of your abundant goodness, and shall sing aloud of your righteousness.

PSALM 145:7 NRSV

You've been planning for months, Pinterest pinned too many times to count. And now that the day is here, the whole family can feel the excitement as you launch final preparations. House cleaned? Check. Balloons inflated? Yes. So now there's just tablecloths to be pressed, centerpieces to be arranged, food to be cooked, candles lit, music selected, and family members prepped for their roles in helping you pull off this party. As the guests arrive, everything falls into place. Soon, you're able to relax and enjoy the fruit of all the effort—the point of all the planning.

Did you know that parties are God's idea? In the Old Testament, we read about several different festivals God designed for His people to celebrate at different times throughout the year. In the New Testament, Jesus explained how the heavenly host celebrates every time a lost soul repents and returns to God. Best of all, He tells us about the all-out, no-holes-barred, literally out-of-this-world celebration He has planned for all His kids when we join Him in heaven. God is planning the party of all parties to celebrate His people joining Him forever.

Parties—the fun of planning and participating—all point to the joy and love flowing from our Father's heart. On top of being holy, righteous, all-powerful, and all-knowing, God is also fun. And He invites you to get excited. He's got surprises in store for today and something spectacular waiting for you in the future. Can you feel the anticipation rising in your soul? Then look for ways to help set the stage, preparing the way for a day, a life, an eternity celebrating God's goodness.

The people of Israel, the priests and the Levites,
and the rest of the returned exiles,
celebrated the dedication of this house of God with joy.

Ezra 6:16 NRSV

NAME CALLING

I am doing this—I, the Lord, the God of Israel, the one who calls you by your name.

ISAIAH 45:3 TLB

It's date night, and you're out at your favorite restaurant, savoring the food and some much-needed fellowship. The hum of conversation happening all around you is a soothing white noise, a pleasant backdrop to your own dialogue unfolding across the dinner table. But suddenly, you stop talking. "Did you hear someone say my name?" you ask. A moment of silence follows, and you both tune your ears to the topics at the other tables. Yes! It's that couple over there, you determine, hearing your name spoken again. But it's clear you've never met them before and conclude they must be talking about someone else.

Isn't it strange how hearing our names can penetrate through all the noise in our lives? It's as if our minds have a special radar solely for detecting someone in the great big universe who actually knows who we are and wants to make a connection. Really, it's a God thing. Our Creator, the One who has a name for every single star, has also named you. You are His child, His treasure, His chosen friend for all eternity. And He calls for connection as you work at your desk, interact with your family at home, drive alone in your car, or sit in a crowded restaurant. If you tune your ears to His heart, you can hear God whisper your name, inviting you to share that moment with Him, to know you are known and loved.

It isn't your imagination. God is beckoning you to come spend time with Him. Tune in to His tender voice this morning and discover a closer connection with Him than you have ever dreamed possible.

He has decided the number of the stars and calls each one by name.

PSALM 147:4 GNT

INTERMISSION

They that wait upon the LORD shall renew their strength.

ISAIAH 40:31 KJV

Warm breezes chased thin white clouds across an azure sky. Golden dandelions danced in the sun as the wind rustled through the tall green grass. What a perfect day it's been, you muse, seated on a hill overlooking the valley not far from your campsite. As you sit and watch the world around you, colors shift to deeper hues. On the horizon, the sun sinks low, painting clouds with deep pinks and oranges as the shadows stretch long on the earth beneath. Even in the changing, the ending, you see an unsung beauty. The world has entered an intermission, the brilliance of day demanding a break until dawn. There is both a sadness and a satisfaction in the day that's been and anticipation for what's yet to come.

Sunsets color more than the skies. They fire our imagination and fill our souls with hope for a beauty that lasts beyond the day. They beckon us to be still, to embrace the necessity of endings to prepare for new beginnings. As much as we resist change and the uncertainty it brings, we see God painting promise for tomorrow every time the sun sets. In His hands, endings are only the temporary pause allowing us rest before even better blessings begin.

Are you nearing a season of change as you rise to greet this new day? Cast your cares on the One who commands the night and ushers in the dawn. Rest in the quiet, and trust God to shine the light on His purpose and plan when the time is right.

What a stack of blessing you have piled up for those who worship you.

PSALM 31:19 THE MESSAGE

SOILED AGAIN

Our light affliction, which is but for a moment, worketh for us a far more exceeding and eternal weight of glory.

2 CORINTHIANS 4:17 KJV

It was only yesterday that the floor had been neatly swept and mopped. But this morning, appearing as if by magic, pawprints of dirt line the floor like a railroad track, recording every filthy footstep your dog made after his trip outside. You groan in frustration as you get the mop, mumbling under your breath about everything that seems to complicate your life, not the least of which is your almost daily battle with the dirt. If only it would just go away, you wish, as you finish up and finally sit down outside to enjoy your morning coffee with some fresh air.

As you relax, you notice God's grand creation—the towering pines and delicate dogwoods; the azaleas and crepe myrtles; even the grass beneath your feet. And a new thought dawns: Dirt anchors all the beauty we see growing above! What seems like a nuisance, a life complication, is really the substance that sustains life's growth. Without dirt, foliage has no foundation. Plants have little source for nutrients. The world as we know it would cease to exist. Dirt is nature's hero.

The same is true for the trials in our lives. Just like dirt, on the surface, our struggles seem intrusive, out of order, something we work hard to sweep out of our lives as soon as possible. But God invites us to see life's circumstances through His eyes. When we do, we see how hard times drive us closer to God, leaning on Him for strength and support. Our spiritual roots grow deeper and stronger into truth when we respond rightly to the trauma of the day. Far from being pointless, our pain provides the surface from which we sink down deeper into God's sustaining grace.

Consider yourselves fortunate when all kinds of trials come your way,
for you know that when your faith succeeds in facing such trials,
the result is the ability to endure.

JAMES 1:2–3 GNT

FALLING *for* YOU

God saw all that He had made, and it was very good. Evening came and then morning: the sixth day.

GENESIS 1:31 HCSB

You felt it the second you stepped out your door this morning: a crisp, cool breeze blew against your skin. The sky overhead seemed a darker blue, the white of the clouds higher and thinner than before. Autumn has arrived, you realize, letting the reality of shifting seasons settle in your mind.

Already you can picture in your mind what lies ahead in the unfolding months. The green foliage of today will give way to dazzling golds and reds, painting the landscape outside your door with royal color. As you recall past fall beauty, you can almost smell the scents of the season, just the thought of spiced apple cider and savory cinnamon making your mouth water in anticipation. And then there's the football games, the roar of the cheers, the comfort of friends gathered around, and the crackle of fire in the fireplace. You've fallen in love with fall. You smile as you savor the moment and then make your way toward your car.

But before the busyness of the day sets in, let your imagination walk one step farther to the Father who brings you the beautiful fall season. The sweep of color and crunch of leaves underfoot are the sights and sounds of God's creative genius, His magnificent painting designed for your pleasure. Like a lover who brings roses to your door, God brings beauty and laughter and life together to demonstrate the depth of His love for you. As you rise this morning, receive life's beauty as His personal gift to you, His invitation to enjoy life in Him, with Him, this day and every day.

I remembered the old days, went over all you've done,
pondered the ways you've worked.

PSALM 143:5 THE MESSAGE

OCEANS DEEP

This hope we have as an anchor of the soul, both sure and steadfast, and which enters the Presence behind the veil.

HEBREWS 6:19 NKJV

It seemed like a fun idea when your friend talked you into it. "Deep sea fishing is amazing. You'll love it!" he promised. As the small charter boat pulled away from the dock into still bay water, familiar sights of seagulls, pelicans, and people lining the shore helped settle your nerves. Soon, though, the scenery changed. Smooth, still water surged in medium-sized swells, rocking the boat left and right as it plunged ahead into what looked like another world entirely.

As you look out in all directions, the dark, deep blue of the ocean and the pale, day sky seals the world in a far-out circle around the tiny boat. Suddenly, the thought dawns: I'm trapped in the middle of an incredibly deep ocean, with no land for safety anywhere in sight. Panic sets in as you nervously peer over the boat's edge to see what creatures may be lurking beneath you. But you paid money for this adventure, and you don't want worry to win. So you bait your hook and drop your line, trusting the friend with you that fun is on its way.

This morning, you may find yourself in the middle of a moment, an event that rocks your world and sends you searching for solid ground. Remember God's promise that everywhere you go, no matter how foreign it feels, God is already there. He made the world, and He made this day for you to trust Him as He calls you into the deeper waters of faith and obedience. Don't let the panic win. Set your soul's anchor in your Father's unfailing love, the only solid ground in life's turbulent waters. And wait with anticipation for today's fun, the catch of the day God has ready for you when you drop your line in trust.

When you pass through deep waters, I will be with you.

ISAIAH 43:2 GNT

SOAK IT IN

Eye has not seen, nor ear heard, nor have entered into the heart of man the things which God has prepared for those who love Him.

1 CORINTHIANS 2:9 NKJV

You've made it! All your hard work and planning have landed you in this spot, plopped down on your beach chair, toes digging into cool, wet sand as the playful surf stretches toward them. Your body responds with a deep breath in, the salt and warmth washing over your weary body. Nature's sights and sounds arrest your senses, and you are struck with wonder: *How can a world so beautiful, so comforting, so soothing, be so real? And why can't this moment last forever?* you wish.

Your heavenly Father smiles at the longing. After all, He spoke the suds and sun into being. He marked the shore's line and sets the seagulls to flight. All that your eyes see and body enjoys are simply a sample from your Father's hand to comfort you now and point you toward an even greater place of permanent joy ahead for you—a place He has been planning and preparing from the beginning of time. God's promised grace now and forever sounds and feels too good to be real. But just as the grains of sand that spread farther than your eyes can see and mind conceive, greater still is the number of thoughts God has of you, His most highly prized creation. His plans to prosper His people are so great you can't even imagine it if you tried, He promises us in His Word.

So today, soak in the warmth of the world of beauty and joy this life affords. And let it well up into an offering of thanks for the forever goodness and grace of God that follows you all the days of your life into greater worlds of love yet to come.

How precious also are Your thoughts to me, O God!
How vast is the sum of them! If I should count them,
they would outnumber the sand.

PSALM 139:17–18 NASB

CROWN *of* GLORY

We do not lose heart, but though our outer man is decaying, yet our inner man is being renewed day by day.

2 CORINTHIANS 4:16 NASB

Your morning had been going like clockwork. Speeding along, your shower's complete, clothes arranged, and you lean in toward the sink to brush your teeth when you notice a new patch of gray sprouting along your crown line. You're not feeling very royal about it. Taking a step back, you look at the image you see before you in the mirror. Oh, it's not the worst, you try to console yourself. But it's not as good as it used to be, the more realistic part of you concedes.

Growing old can be a pain—literally. Nuisances like graying hairs and handles you don't love at all are one thing. But add to it the wrinkles, the aches and pains, even the eyesight giving way and you can't help but complain at least a little. Why doesn't beauty last? Why hasn't science figured out how to reverse the aging process for good? The good news is that God does have a reverse process happening inside you. Though the outside is "wasting away," as the Bible puts it, God is steadily at work in our hearts, changing our minds and shaping our souls into His beautiful image. Though it may not feel like it, in God's eyes we are becoming more beautiful with every passing day.

As for that body that can be such a bother at times, don't let it get to you. Remember that you get to exchange it for a perfect one that never grows old when you get to heaven. But for now, your sags and soreness can just be your signal that you're one day closer to perfection and fully loved by God in the process.

Bless the LORD, O my soul ... who satisfies your years
with good things, so that your youth is renewed like the eagle.

PSALM 103:2–5 NASB

Let me hear of your unfailing love
each morning, for I am trusting you.
Show me where to walk,
for I give myself to you.

PSALM 143:8 NLT

As *by* Fire

*Endure trials for the sake of discipline. God is treating you as
children; for what child is there whom a parent does not discipline?*

HEBREWS 12:7 NRSV

From the base of the trunk, you can barely see to the top. Like mammoth spears plunged into the ground, thousands of ruddy, rough trunks line up across the landscape and shoot straight up into the sky. Foliage found way above blocks out much of the sunlight, casting cool shadows on the forest floor far below. It's a magical feel in the forest of Redwood National Park. Home to the world's tallest trees, it's easy to feel small, even insignificant surrounded by such overarching beauty.

But beside one of the trees you can also find a sign explaining the growth process. As these trees grow, so do the weeds and underbrush that threaten to steal much-needed nutrients from the soil. Left unchecked, the underbrush becomes the great Redwood's undoing. But as God would have it, lightning periodically ignites fires that burn through the forest. The stronger Redwoods withstand the heat, though the blazes often leave scars. But the undergrowth doesn't burns away, and the Redwood is free to reach even higher toward heaven.

In a similar way, God allows the right kind of fires in our lives. These fires are perfectly designed to burn up the weeds that are choking out our love for Him. Maybe we lose a job or a home. Maybe our kids rebel in ways we never thought they would. Maybe our marriage falls apart, or we get a bad diagnosis. These fires are always painful. But through it we grow stronger and closer to God if we stay rooted in His love, trusting His eternal purpose.

See to it that no one fails to obtain the grace of God;
that no root of bitterness springs up and causes trouble.

HEBREWS 12:15 NRSV

RIDING ROLLER COASTERS

When we were children, we thought and reasoned as children do. But when we grew up, we quit our childish ways.

1 CORINTHIANS 13:11 CEV

Before you even find your seat, your heart is already racing in anticipation. Inside, you pull the harness down tight. You worry as you feel a little give in the lock. But you don't have time to analyze because the ride has started, and you know there's no going back. Jerking you into alignment, the cars make the telltale click as they slowly climb what seems to be straight up into the air. At long last, you teeter at the top for just a second. Suddenly, the cars pull you straight down into certain death (or so it feels) as your stomach and head revolt against such madness. Strangely, at the same time as all the terror, a silly smile lines your face. This is terrible and tremendous, tragic and terrific, all at the same time!

And so it goes, not only on rollercoasters, but also in life. The highs and lows even in a single day can send your heart racing, emotions surging from anger to ecstasy in a matter of minutes. Thank God for the emotions! Emotions are a gift that helps connect us to God and others. They let us know we're human, and very much alive. But they aren't reliable drivers in the ride.

When we acknowledge that God alone directs our course and stay connected to Him—just like rollercoaster cars always keep on track—we can stay anchored even through the rises and falls of life. The twists and turns in life can be scary and exhilarating, nerve-wracking and incredible, unpredictable and delightful. Through it all, we can smile, knowing we're held all the while by the strong, certain, and unbreakable grip of God. So today, sit back and enjoy the ride!

He will order his angels to protect you wherever you go.
They will hold you up with their hands
so you won't even hurt your foot on a stone.

PSALM 91:11-12 NLT

STAR *of* WONDER

God saw that the light was good. Then he separated the light from the darkness.

GENESIS 1:4 NLT

Have you ever wondered what it's like where the stars live? Not the celebrity kind, but the celestial sort—those curious, gleaming beams of light we see shining through the darkness of our night? Can you imagine getting closer? The brightness and burning would be so intense that you couldn't describe it. A ball of surging power, radiating a glory as it sits alone, suspended in space. Though deepest darkness lies all around, its light shines greater, sending energy in waves countless light years away.

What a miracle each star is! What a wonder that God would compare us to each of these. Yet He did. When we look up at the night sky, we witness God's picture of His people, lives filled with the glory of His incredible power and brilliance. Burning with a supernatural passion for real beauty and truth, we stand out in the darkness of this world. And for some who come near, our fire is too bright, too intense for them. With no light of their own, the lost often prefer the darkness. But don't be discouraged. Starlight also illuminates our world and lights the way for those who recognize their need.

Today, as you rise up for the occasion of life, fuel up on the power of God's Word. Invite His Spirit inside you to chase away any shadows of self or the darkness of doubt, and let His love wash over the world around you and illuminate it with His wonderful light.

Live clean, innocent lives as children of God,
shining like bright lights
in a world full of crooked and perverse people.

PHILIPPIANS 2:15 NLT

WRAPPED UP

Take away my sin, and I will be clean. Wash me, and I will be whiter than snow.

PSALM 51:7 NCV

It has been a long, hard day. It feels like you've literally walked miles to and from the millions of errands you take care of for home and work, your pedometer confirming your suspicions. All you want to do now is take a shower, put on your PJs, and climb into bed, in that order. And you do just that. Only you have a pleasant surprise waiting for you as you pull back the covers: clean sheets. How could something so simple feel so spectacular? Sliding in, your body embraces the cool, silky sensation, and you can't help but rub your legs back and forth across the smooth surface. With cleanness all around, it's easy to unwind and usher in the sleep you so desperately need.

There's just something special about being clean and wrapped up in it. It feels right. Maybe even what we're born—and destined—for. In the Bible, John relays the vision he saw in heaven, that of a vast sea of people praising God and waving palm branches. The angel next to John explained that those people were God's family, all those who have trusted in Jesus to wash their souls white as snow. And now, standing before the very throne of Almighty God, they were given robes, washed perfectly white with God's own righteousness. They were all clean and wrapped up in their robes, thanks to God's glorious grace.

As you get up this morning, meditate on your destiny. One day you will stand spotless and perfectly clean before God's throne if you have put your faith in Jesus. You are destined for perfection and will revel and rest in the Savior's cleansing sensation.

The LORD rewarded me because I did what was right, because I did what the LORD said was right.

PSALM 18:24 NCV

BURNING LOVE

Let's not get tired of doing what is good. At just the right time we will reap a harvest of blessing if we don't give up.

GALATIANS 6:9 NLT

It may be cold outside, but in here, snuggled on the couch with a cozy blanket and a crackling fire in the fireplace, it's toasty warm and oh-so-comfortable! So you pull out your favorite book and begin to read, reveling in the relaxation and comfort the moment affords. Before too long, though, you notice a bit more of a chill in the air. Looking up from the page, you notice the fire has died down, now curling quietly over the last remaining logs. You wrap the blanket around you a little tighter and plunge ahead in the plot, the most intense part just a chapter or two away. But before you get there, the fire goes out altogether. Suddenly, the room seems far less romantic, far colder, and clearly in some serious need of attention if you want the heart- and body-warming ambience to continue.

The same is true for our relationships. Like the fire in the fireplace, they only produce heat and warmth when you put the necessary work into them. But they are not static. Neglected, they are destined to diminish. Ignore them long enough, and they will die out completely. So God urges you to keep the fire burning in your relationships—with Him, your spouse, and everyone God has put in your life to love and serve. Resist the temptation to let life coast along or become too distracted by the day's drama, and you will reap great rewards in your soul and life.

This morning, ask God to give you creativity, perseverance, and determination to keep up the good work of cultivating strong relationships with others.

Love never gives up, never loses faith, is always hopeful, and endures through every circumstance.

1 CORINTHIANS 13:7 NLT

BREATHE IN

This is what God the LORD says—the Creator of the heavens ... who gives breath to its people, and life to those who walk on it.

ISAIAH 42:5 NIV

Take a deep breath in, the doctor instructs. You comply as she readjusts her stethoscope to hear different places around your lungs. "Now breathe out." You exhale, waiting to hear about any discoveries she may have made while the oxygen exchange was taking place. It's important to make sure the lungs are functioning properly. The quality and amount of oxygen you process with every breath in has a direct impact on the way the rest of your body functions.

When you stop to think about it, breathing itself is its own miracle—one that happens anywhere from 17,000 to 30,000 times a day, depending on your age! In order to keep on living, laughing, talking, and loving, we have to keep on breathing. It's the way God designed for us to get the energy from the outside to the inside of us, fueling our bodies as needed. It's a second-by-second reminder of our critical reliance upon the divine breath of God who brings us life in the first place. Should He want to, God could withdraw His breath from His creatures, and all life would instantly cease. Fortunately, He wants the opposite: to fill His people with His breath of life—not only to keep your physical heart pumping and body running, but also to fill you with His Spirit so you can live this life to its fullest.

When you breathe in deeply by reading and believing His Word, you are filled with supernatural energy, joy, and power to exhale God's amazing grace into the world around you. This morning, take a deep breath, drawing on God's incredible goodness and love for you. Then look for all the ways God brings you today to breathe out His grace everywhere you go.

The heavens were made by the word of the LORD, and all the stars,
by the breath of His mouth.

PSALM 33:6 HCSB

CENTER STAGE

For you that honor my name, victory will shine like the sun with healing in its rays

MALACHI 4:2 CEV

When you awoke this morning, it was peeking through your windows. Once you are outside, though, all formalities are gone. The sun bears down, casting its rays full force onto you and everything around you. It's so bright that you involuntarily shield your eyes, hand cupped over forehead, as you look at all the beauty lit up by its brilliance. It's going to be another gorgeous day, and you can't wait to get going in it.

But before you do, take a moment to soak up a powerful truth along with the sun's rays. God, who made this reliable source of energy for all the Earth's needs, didn't place our planet in the center for the sun to circle around us. Instead, the sun takes center stage, and we spin precariously through

space at just the right distance to receive blessing instead of burns from the sun's massive output of energy.

Likewise, God has also given us His Son, Jesus, the source of energy for all things, including stars and planets. We do not demand that God cater to us, orbiting around our small worlds, insisting that everything happen the way we please. No, we understand our rightful place when our lives are orbiting around the Son of God. With proper perspective of Who's in the center, we find ourselves poised at every angle to reap the healing warmth and power of His love.

Today, do you need to realign your thinking to become more God-centered than self-centered? If so, confess it to God and ask Him for wisdom from above. Let the light of His love shine down full force into your soul to keep your life anchored in orbit around Him.

From east to west, the powerful LORD God has been calling together everyone on earth.

PSALM 50:1 CEV

Reflections

In returning and rest you shall be saved; in quietness and in trust shall be your strength.

Isaiah 30:15 NRSV

Not a breeze is blowing. Only the sound of crickets stirs the thick summer air as you step up to the sandy lake shore. Looking out, you almost lose your breath. Languid water and hazy blue sky pose as mirrors, the image and colors of the heavens reflecting so perfectly on the stillness below that you can't even discern where one ends and the other begins. It's just a palette of blues in differing hues, dotted by clouds. But as fish break the surface and ripples roll across the lake, the illusion is lost and the unyielding sky wins.

The truth is, reflections are seen best in the stillness. It is why God calls out to His very busy creatures to, "Be still, and know that I am God." While we carry on the frantic pace of our lives, we miss the beauty of all that is above.

We worry, we stress, we plan, we manipulate, we labor long to make life work the way we think it should when all along we'd be better off being still and reflecting the beauty of the heavens.

Today, take time to be still. Sit in silence before the God who made you and knows you. Listen for the still, small voice that tells you what your heart really needs to know for this day. When you take time to sit still in God's glorious presence, you take on His image—a work of beauty that will take the world's breath away.

Be still, and know that I am God! I am exalted among the nations,
I am exalted in the earth.

PSALM 46:10 NRSV

MORNING MIRACLES

In him we live, and move, and have our being; as certain also of your own poets have said, for we are also his offspring.

ACTS 17:28 KJV

It's a miracle if you get out of bed this morning, not because you're desperately wanting to sleep longer, either. Marvel, for just a moment, about how God has wired your body. Without as much as a conscious thought, your heart has continued beating and your lungs breathing all throughout the night and carries on even as you read your morning devotional. In order to pick up this book, the bones in your body worked in tandem with muscles perfectly connected to make motion happen. Nerve endings and sense of touch and sight sent signals to your brain which almost instantaneously assessed the data and reacted with a command for your hand to open, close, and retrieve the book you wanted to read.

And so it goes with everything we see, say, and do. We

are living, breathing, miraculous acts of God. And as Paul explained it, we live and move and have our being in God. The source of all this magnificent biological technology that we most often take for granted is our Creator, who designed us perfectly to live this life in grateful devotion to the One who sustains our every moment.

So take a deep breath. Wriggle your toes. Notice the fine prints on every finger. And realize that this day—and your life in it—is a miraculous gift from God, not to be taken lightly. Thank Him for creating you exactly as He did, and for His amazing grace that keeps you going day after day. Then ask Him to fill you so that He can use your physical frame, as well as your heart, mind, and soul, to bring Him the glory He is due this day.

You protect me with your saving shield. You support me with your right hand. You have stooped to make me great.

PSALM 18:35 NCV

TRAINING DAY

No day will pass without its reward as you mature in your experience of our Master Jesus.

2 PETER 1:8 THE MESSAGE

Anyone would have been impressed, the way that dog on stage followed its owner's every command on cue. Pet owners know that training of that caliber doesn't come easy. Time, repetition, consistency, and relevant rewards for right behavior are crucial for training success. But what about us? What is the motivation for making right decisions? We don't have people around us popping treats in our mouths every time we choose to behave in a God-honoring way. What is the motivation today to do what is right?

The same God who wired animal brains designed ours in a similar, though higher-functioning fashion. We, too, can train our minds to think and respond according to our Master's commands, the process developing through a system of rewards. Only the rewards don't come out of a store-bought bag. They come from God's presence in our lives. God tells us in His Word that when we seek after Him with all of our hearts, He rewards us with a richer, deeper, stronger relationship. Generous gifts sown toward His kingdom reap lasting pleasure as we discover our God-given purpose in this world while storing up riches in heaven. Suddenly, to act in ways against God's nature just seems empty. Pointless. Offensive even. We begin to live for the reward we know is surely coming. God is giving us more of Himself every time we choose to follow Him.

Today, as you walk out onto the stage of your life, will you surrender to the Master as He trains your soul in righteousness? He wants to retrain your brain to obey the One who brings the richest rewards.

If you do what is right, you are certain to be rewarded.

PROVERBS 11:18 GNT

I have scattered your offenses
like the morning mist.
Oh, return to me,
for I have paid the price
to set you free.

ISAIAH 44:22 NLT

TOUCHED *by* LOVE

The one with human likeness touched me again and strengthened me.

DANIEL 10:18 HCSB

You were able to hold it together up until this point. Though sadness had seeped deep into your soul, you steeled yourself to keep all appearances steady. But your friend blew your cover with the simple, caring touch of her hand. Seeing the tears welling in your eyes, she hugged you hard and firm, the softness of her concern shattering the dam holding back the emotional torrent now surging through your entire body. How can a single touch yield such tremendous power? How can a hug demolish all defenses?

When we feel loved, when we tangibly sense the touch of another person, connection happens. Not just the kind between giver and receiver, but a sense of your heavenly

Father's deepest affection flows through the current, healing both souls. For whatever reason, God has chosen people, His people, to be the physical vessels through which His Spirit pours, the literal hands and feet of God's own body to serve and save the world. When we reach out to those who are hurting, we are living conduits of God's grace and love. And when we receive hands laid on us for prayer, encouragement, and support, we receive the embrace of God.

Do you ever wonder if God loves you? Do you ever wish He'd just appear and prove His love is real? Remember, God sent His Son so we could see in human form what real love is. Then He sent His Spirit to live inside His children, so we can feel, receive, and give that love to others. As you prepare for your day, ask yourself who in your life could use God's touch of love today. Then make it happen.

Jesus came up, touched them, and said, "Get up; don't be afraid."

MATTHEW 17:7 HCSB

ARTISTIC LICENSE

God gives us many kinds of special abilities, but it is the same
Holy Spirit who is the source of them all.

1 CORINTHIANS 12:4 TLB

The art teacher stood in front of the class, satisfied that she had given her students all the directions they needed. The living model was sitting as still as possible in full view of all. "My objective for this assignment is to see your perspective," she concluded. After time passed, the teacher slowly walked down each aisle and surveyed each student's work. *What a pleasant surprise*, she thought. No one had drawn the entire man. Instead, each student accented a different part, with some adding imaginative twists all their own. The resulting amalgam of artistic license took the teacher's breath away. One single model had inspired an entire world of creativity.

Such creative genius isn't just for the artistically inclined. Each of us offers a unique perspective, a delightfully different personality through which the love and grace of God can flow. The idea that all Christians should look and act the same way is as boring a thought as a duplicate art piece. The wonder and beauty of creativity stems from the Creator who gives it to us. When we approach the people and circumstances of life confident in who God created us specifically to be, we usher breathtaking beauty and perspective into this world.

As you enjoy the beauty of this fresh, new morning, thank God for wiring you exactly the way He did. Ask Him to help you be yourself, filled with His Spirit, inspired by His creativity, ready to paint your world with the creative perspective that only you can give.

He has made many parts for our bodies
and has put each part just where he wants it.

1 CORINTHIANS 12:18 TLB

LOST *in* TRANSLATION

May our Lord Jesus Christ ... comfort your hearts with all comfort, and help you in every good thing you say and do.

2 THESSALONIANS 2:16–17 TLB

Y ou've had it happen before and swore you wouldn't repeat the mistake. At the moment, it seemed like texting your thoughts would simplify the situation. After all, you had time to think and craft your words before pressing "send." But seeing the reply, you sensed a signal got crossed. Words meant for explanation wounded the recipient instead. Strangely, you could feel the tension, even through the text. Immediately you choose to switch modes, clicking the call button instead. Real conversation ensues, and the miscommunications get sorted out. Tragedy averted. Relationship restored.

Good communication can be tricky no matter what mode we use. But words are not the only part of communication people choose to read. How we say what we say and the hidden motivation behind our comments carry even deeper meaning. God calls His kids to be strong communicators for His kingdom's sake. He reminds us throughout His Word that the world is watching—and reading—our lives. Any discrepancy between how we talk and how we live speaks volumes. Do we say we love God but fail to help those in need? Do we like our church but sit out when they request help? Do we tell others we'll pray for them but not with them in the moment? Though we may not mean for it to happen, the reality of God's love and presence gets lost in our contradicting translation.

This morning, ask God to help you sync the story of your mouth with the plot of your life. Be the salt and light God has called you to be, leading others closer to Him in every kind of conversation.

Little children, let us stop just saying we love people;
let us really love them, and show it by our actions.

1 JOHN 3:18 TLB

BORN *to* BE BEAUTIFUL

While the king is on his couch, my perfume releases its fragrance.

SONG OF SONGS 1:12 HCSB

He had it hidden behind his back so you couldn't see. Still, you smelled a sweetness even while he stood at your door. Then, with a smile on his face and outstretched arm, he revealed his hidden treasure: a dozen red roses wrapped tightly at the stems, bow flowing down. Instinctively, you bent over and breathed in the scent, even before accepting the beautiful offering. Flattered and humbled, you couldn't help but blush as you bring the bouquet inside.

Isn't it amazing how something as simple as flowers can bring the world such beauty and joy? What starts out as a tiny seed planted deep in the dirt simply grows over time. Sun, water, and soil work a mysterious magic, splitting the hull and sending shoots straight toward the sky. In time, the tall green of the stems yield to the crowning bud, where color and fragrance infuse delicate petals, soft and curled around each other with stunning precision.

In a similar way, God is growing each of His people up into unimaginable beauty that makes this world a better and brighter place. Every day that we soak up the rich nutrients of His love and truth, our roots grow deeper, stems stronger as we grow up in Him. And as we grow, a deeper mystery unfolds. Our lives soften. Our thoughts and words and actions grow sweeter. And we become the very fragrance of Christ, God's beautiful gift of love to the world He wants to win over.

Today, don't grow impatient with yourself or your circumstances. Instead, understand that God's growing beauty in you is in process. Stay rooted in Him, and you can be sure that your life, God's gift, will bless the world around you.

God uses us to make the knowledge about Christ
spread everywhere like a sweet fragrance.

2 Corinthians 2:14 GNT

The RIGHT MIX

It is pleasant to see plans develop.

PROVERBS 13:19 TLB

It tasted so good at the party, you knew you'd have to try baking it yourself at home. But now that your friend has sent over the recipe, you're a little dumbfounded. Staples like sugar and flour you certainly recognize. But some of the spice requirements stop you in your tracks. Heading to the most gourmet grocery near you, you scan the spice rack until you find the special ingredients your recipe calls for. Back at home, you begin measuring, mixing, blending, noting that even the order of instructions seems counterintuitive to your cooking experience. Yet you stick to the script, following directions, trusting that in the end you will produce the same delicious dessert you first tasted at the party. In the end, you are delighted with the results.

Life is like a big mixing bowl filled with very different ingredients. Part of the mix is sweet. But other events and circumstances can add quite a bitter edge. It's hard not to question some of the trials and challenges God incorporates into the lump of dough that is your life. The ingredients and the process often seem out of order and completely counterintuitive to how you would have written the recipe. But if we want to taste the heavenly delight in the end, we need to stick to God's script. Keep living according to His Word, trusting that He will work both the sweet and the unsavory into one complete dish worth serving to the world and pleasing to Him.

Today, as you taste different foods throughout your day, remember that God's goodness and control bring purpose to the process. He is bringing exactly the right mix of people and circumstances needed to make you the person He created you to be.

Take firm hold of instruction, do not let go; keep her, for she is your life.

PROVERBS 4:13 NKJV

FOREVER FAMILY

God decided in advance to adopt us into his own family by bringing us to himself through Jesus Christ.

EPHESIANS 1:5 NLT

For years they had waited, hoped, prayed, and spent money, time, and countless tears as they wrestled through mountains of paperwork and jumped through every government-required hoop. As months turned into years, faith mingled with fear: fear of the country closing adoptions, fear that the child they loved sight unseen would never make it home. But then it came in the mail. It was only a single photo of their child with a short description beside it, but to the couple it was their hope reborn. Yet even that moment paled in comparison to the one when they finally met, face to face, eye to eye. At last, they were family.

All the struggle, cost, and completed joy adoption brings helps us see our Father's heart. We were spiritual orphans, desperately needing a home. He could have ignored us, made us slaves or even guests, but He didn't. He wanted more. God wanted a family—children with whom He could share His love and home. Though sin had separated us from Him, God relentlessly labored to bring His children home, the cost He paid in Jesus infinitely higher than any earthly fee.

This morning as you prepare for the day, consider all the preparations God made so you could be His own child. You are no outsider to His love, affection, power, and riches. Everything He has and all He is was given to you the moment you accepted His invitation to life with Him. Joined together with every believer, we now celebrate the largest family of brothers and sisters this world has ever seen. And we will never be separated again.

You are citizens with everyone else who belongs to the family of God.

Ephesians 2:19 CEV

CUTTING EDGE

Faithful are the wounds of a friend.

PROVERBS 27:6 NKJV

You couldn't believe it. You had been carrying on, laughing and joking like you usually do. But then your friend called you out. Even worse, she admitted she had given thought, even prayer to the problem. Dumbfounded, you listened long enough to learn that she actually believed you had sin in your soul, a blind spot that surfaced whenever you spoke about a particular person you both know. Her words cut like a knife, and you recoiled from the wound. Thoughts flooded your mind as you mentally mounted a strong defense against her accusation. I do not gossip! I'm only telling the truth, you rebutted. Then you thought, *And who is she to tell me I talk badly about others?* But then her smile disrupted your mental tirade before the words escaped your lips. "You know I love you, right?" she asked. And on

second thought, you remembered that she indeed did. That she actually was kind. And maybe, just maybe, she was right.

As painful as it may be at times, God often corrects His kids through others. Left to our own devices, we simply tend to gloss over our weaknesses. But God loves us and the world around us too much to let us inhibit our spiritual growth. So He gives us spouses, teachers, and close friends who will risk telling us the truth, people who are willing to navigate the turbulent waters of our tempers so we can be free.

And freedom is the result of a blind spot surrendered. Once it is seen, we can confess and be cleansed, bound no longer by that secret sin's power. This day, ask God to help you receive His correction, in whatever form it comes, with a humble and listening heart.

No chastening seems to be joyful for the present, but painful; nevertheless, afterward it yields the peaceable fruit of righteousness.

HEBREWS 12:11 NKJV

155

SAKURA BLOOMS

The grass withers, and its flower falls away, but the word of the LORD endures forever.

1 PETER 1:24–25 NKJV

It's early April, and already the delicate pink blooms of the sakura, Japanese cherry trees, have burst into billowy color. Tens of thousands of tourists have converged on the nation's capital, eager to see the softness of willowy beauty amid sobering stone memorials. The landscape does not disappoint. For a brief couple of weeks, the city grounds are awash in pastel glory, the cherry blossoms accentuating the noble and heroic feats of all the lives lived and lost for a cause greater than themselves.

And then, just like that, the glory fades. The petals fall, and the world moves on. The transient display of the beautiful Sakura trees tell a story just as profound as the words and historical scenes that populate the city: Even the greatest leaders do not lead forever. Soldiers, prisoners, civilians, politicians flourish or flounder in the brevity of their lives. They, like all of us, are here today, but gone tomorrow. Those who lived for something greater than themselves, however, left a lasting legacy for those coming behind. A life lived with the joy of heaven in mind brings lasting impact here on earth. God's Word alone will stand the test of time, as will all those who base their faith and actions on it.

This morning, may the sobering thought of life's inevitable brevity make you bold. There's no time to waste. Live life to its fullest with God and His eternal riches in view as you ask Him to establish His order for your day.

Lay up for yourselves treasures in heaven, where neither moth nor rust destroys and where thieves do not break in and steal.

MATTHEW 6:20 NKJV

GREATER

*If our conscience condemns us, we know that God is greater than
our conscience and that he knows everything.*

1 JOHN 3:20 GNT

Unable to sleep, you decide to walk off dinner and
the normal jitters you feel when you travel. At the
short boardwalk over the dunes, you ditch your shoes and
soon sink your toes into the now cool, soft sand, the golden
glow of day now washed in night grays. Silence settles in,
except the gentle rhythmic lapping of the shoreline at your
feet. Alone, the quiet calms your soul, and you breathe in
the bigness of it all: black night sky and deep, dark ocean
accentuate the smallness of your frame. All the important
matters of the day, of your life, seem lost in the vastness of
the universe above and around you. In the grand scheme
of all that is, you wonder why you even matter, how your
life can possibly make a difference in this overwhelming

cosmos.

But in the stillness, a small voice with the power of a thousand suns reminds you of a young boy's lunch given long ago. A small meal surrendered into the Master's hands became life and nourishment for an entire multitude. He was only a child. It was just one meal. But in the surrender, God made a miracle of eternal impact. On your own, your life may very well be a simple drop in the ocean. But when that drop is surrendered to God's almighty presence and power within you, He brings eternal purpose to even the smallest acts of love you do.

Today, as you face the enormity of all that comes your way, remember that God is so much bigger. He will empower you to make the difference you are destined to make for this day.

He has spoken to us through his Son.
He is the one through whom God created the universe.

HEBREWS 1:2 GNT

LOVE SONGS

The LORD your God is in your midst. ... He will exult over you with joy, He will be quiet in His love.

ZEPHANIAH 3:17 NASB

The second it comes on the radio, your heart soars—it's your all-time, hands-down favorite love song. Without a second thought, you crank it up in your car loud enough to be heard from outside, but inside you've let the music and melody take you to that special place in your mind it always does. Through those notes and lyrics, you imagine another place and time where you reveled in the affection and attraction of some other, a place where you are free to not only be yourself, but to be fully loved as the quirky and unique person you are. For the three minutes the song plays, you are in your perfect paradise. Of course, when the song ends, the day's realities resume.

Romantic notions of hope and deep connection get shelved for another day, perhaps another song. In real life, your experience tells you that even the best, most enduring loves might not last, at least not with the unbridled passion of youth. In real life you have to settle for a love that's more, well, down to earth. Or do you?

Maybe that's exactly the problem with an earth-bound love. We were made for more. We were designed to know and be known on the deepest levels of our souls. Did you know that the God who created you sings love songs over you as well? His attraction and commitment to you rivals none. He alone can satisfy our aching souls with the kind of connection we all truly crave. Unlike love songs on the radio, God's singing for you started before He made the world, and His delight in you doesn't fade away. It welcomes you to stay in His presence and revel in His love now and forever.

To those who are the called, beloved in God the Father,
and kept for Jesus Christ: May mercy and peace and love
be multiplied to you.

JUDE 1-2 NASB

The Lord's love never ends;
his mercies never stop.
They are new every morning

LAMENTATIONS 3:22–23 NCV

CHOSEN

GOD judges persons differently than humans do. Men and women look at the face; GOD looks into the heart.

1 SAMUEL 16:7 THE MESSAGE

The team captains stood in front of the PE class, surveying the assortment of gym-shorts clad potentials before them. Those who were confident in their athletic reputation simply wondered if they'd be picked first. But the others, those who knew their talents lay elsewhere, just dreaded the process. Of course they wouldn't be picked—at least not until everyone better had been snatched up. For some of them, it was the story of their lives. Being the one chosen simply never happened. Not in PE, not ever.

Fearing rejection follows us far beyond the travails of childhood. Even into our golden years, it's hard to grasp our true value and worth with all the ways the world has to bring us down. Yet God surveys the playing field quite differently. Far from the team captain who chooses the one who is smartest, fastest, and brightest, God often chooses the weakest, the neediest, the ones desperate for His divine help to live and achieve His purposes. Over every asset our culture deems important, God chooses the humble.

This morning, if you find yourself feeling too weak and too inadequate for what lies ahead, you are in the perfect place to be snatched up by the team captain and placed in the starting line-up. Take your need to the only One who can give you the power and strength you need. Humbly submit to His Spirit's coaching, and you can be certain He will choose you to be on His team, ready to win the world to Him by His mighty power.

Your servant is in the midst of Your people whom You have chosen,
a great people, too numerous to be numbered or counted.

1 KINGS 3:8 NKJV

FULL FORCE

There is now no condemnation awaiting those who belong to Christ Jesus.

You open the drawer and let out a deep sigh as you reach for sweatpants again. After all the festivities and food from the holidays, it's just expected, you rationalize. But it doesn't make the New Year's leaf any easier to turn over. You know what it's going to take to get back into your better-looking wardrobe: a lot of work. So you set your mind to the goal and begin anew. For a week, you stick to your plan, but week two is another story. It seems like every temptation possible is testing your resolve. Before long your resolution melts away instead of the weight you intended to lose. *Why are the simple things so hard to do?* you wonder.

The apostle Paul says we're in a fight. He probably didn't have a scale in mind, but he did know that our bodies are often at odds with our hearts. We desire to do well physically, emotionally, and spiritually, but another part of our person seems to have other plans. When we fail, it's so easy to want to give up. But God, through the words of Paul, sets us free. Even when our own hearts condemn us, God does not. He has declared His people to be perfect in His sight, simply because we belong to Him. So we stay in the fight—the fight to believe God's power to declare us perfect and the fight to fend off the fleshly desires that would keep us from becoming all God created us to be.

As you start your day, remember that you are perfectly loved and sustained by God's grace. Then pray for His power to fight off everything that hinders you from feeling its full force

I have fought a good fight, I have finished my course,
I have kept the faith.

2 TIMOTHY 4:7 KJV

BEAUTIFUL SOLES

The Scriptures say, "How beautiful are the feet of messengers who bring good news!"

ROMANS 10:15 NLT

You probably hardly ever notice them, but they're with you everywhere you go. Every stair you climb. Every trip you take. There, at the end of your legs, are the two most important tools for your personal transportation. Whether you're walking, jogging, jumping, or simply standing, your own two feet have to toe the line every time. And when they don't—when injury or illness impairs—life takes on a whole new level of difficulty. You and I—we all need our feet!

In fact, God says our feet are beautiful. They take us to the people who need to hear about hope. They walk us away from our comfort zones to those places of need where others won't go. God gives us feet so we can carry

His blessing beyond our own borders into the waiting world beyond. Best of all, God promises to direct our steps to those very places and people where we need to go. God could have chosen to keep Jesus here on earth ministering from village to village as He did while on earth. But God had bigger plans. In fact, Jesus told His followers that it was best that He return to heaven so that His Spirit could come and fill all believers with His presence. Now He works through us, physically and practically bringing God's hope, joy, and love into every life we touch, every hand we hold, every hug we give.

God is calling you, this morning, to go for a walk! Let His Spirit lead you into all the ways He has planned for you to minister to others in His name. You are God's expression of love for others, and it is beautiful!

Shapely and graceful your sandaled feet. …
Your limbs are lithe and elegant, the work of a master artist.

SONG OF SONGS 7:1 THE MESSAGE

GARDEN GROWTH

The seed that fell on good soil represents those who truly hear and understand God's word and produce a harvest of thirty, sixty, or even a hundred times as much as had been planted!

MATTHEW 13:23 NLT

She led you through the halls of her humble home until she reached the back door where she welcomed you to walk ahead. As you pushed open the door, it took a moment for your eyes to take in the beautiful scene that spread before you. Nestled inside the old brick fence lining the perimeter of her property grew the most spectacular garden you had ever seen. A graceful weeping willow kept the corner guard, with dozens of daffodils standing at attention, all swaying slightly in the warm spring breeze. Brilliant pink and red peonies, encore azaleas, and a variety of ferns and tall grasses lined the pebbled pathway through the hand-wrought paradise. It was obvious the owner was proud of her handiwork. "What's your secret?" you wondered aloud as you inhaled the varied fragrances. Smiling, she answered, "The secret's in the soil."

Before she ever planted a single bulb, she had tilled the soil and tested the quality. Much of it required additional nutrients before the conditions were ripe for planting. But rooted in the right soil, beautiful growth was inevitable. Our hearts are much like our gardens. We may all hear the message of truth about God's grace and forgiveness, but only hearts that are tilled with humility and repentance are seasoned properly to receive those spiritual seeds. When we are open to receive God's grace, acknowledging our desperate need for Him, the light of His Son streams down, the richness of truth fills up, and our lives sprout up in beautiful display of His magnificent handiwork.

This morning, ask God to tend to the soil of your soul. Then watch in wonder at the beautiful growth God will bring to your life.

It was already planted in good soil and had plenty of water so it could grow into a splendid vine and produce rich leaves and luscious fruit.

EZEKIEL 17:8 NLT

171

SEASONED

Your speech should always be gracious, seasoned with salt, so that you may know how you should answer each person.

COLOSSIANS 4:6 HCSB

You've been working on the stew for hours and have followed the recipe exactly as prescribed. But as you dip the spoon into the promising liquid and take a sip, you're taken aback. Despite the vivid color and even aroma, the soup base itself is far too bland for your liking. So you break out even more spices, adding some fresh-cut basil, ground cumin, and a little curry for good measure. Then you cap off your seasoning frenzy with a healthy dose of salt and black pepper. Swirling it into the liquid, you hope for the best and give it another taste. *Ah ... perfection!* You smile. Now the look, smell, and taste all work together to make your stew a hall-of-fame winner for your family.

God says that more than just good soups need seasoning. Our lives require even more. It's one thing to say we are Christians and give the appearance of being good, moral, upstanding people. But without a real relationship with the Creator, our lives are bland, watered down, and without the power needed to please God or give others a taste of what He's like. So God uses trials and difficulties to season our souls, enriching the depth of our life's flavor as we learn to depend solely on Him for strength, forgiveness, righteousness, and hope. His spice blend is different for each of us, but it always produces His desired effect.

When you yield to the Master Chef, your life—struggles and triumphs—will produce a depth of character that can truly feed and nourish others with God's goodness. As you prepare for the day, ask God to season your conversations with His grace and deepen your taste and experience of His love.

You are the salt of the earth. But if the salt should lose its taste,
how can it be made salty?

MATTHEW 5:13 HCSB

FLYING HIGH

[God] sent from above, he took me, he drew me out of many waters. ... He brought me forth also into a large place; he delivered me, because he delighted in me.

PSALM 18:16,19 KJV

At least you don't panic at the thought of flying. But now that you're thousands of feet in the air in the middle of a violent thunderstorm, there's a knot in your stomach. Instinctively you tighten your seatbelt and peer out your small porthole window, willing the plane to land safely. Instead, you're amazed by the density of thick, dark clouds whirling past your window at breakneck speed. You understand there's nothing you can do to save yourself. You'll have to trust the pilot you can't see and the plane with mechanisms you can't fully understand. After a series of tumultuous turns and sudden drops, you catch the faint sight of blue and yellow runway lights. Then you hear the landing gear engage. Before you know it, the plane has touched down and come to a stop. At last you can exhale, giving thanks to the pilot and God for His grace.

It's uncanny how similar our lives are to airplane rides. We may think we're in control of where we're going and how we get there, but there are some serious limits to what God enables us to do. As the true Pilot, He directs our course and keeps us safe. He can see into the dark places and turbulent air masses with ease. No matter how scary it may seem and how many surprise bumps we experience, we can still soar through life with true peace when our lives are completely in His loving, capable hands.

This morning, don't let panic steal your joy. Remember that if you have chosen God as your Pilot, you will reach His destination for you safely. You are free to enjoy the view and comfort those around you who don't yet fly with God's higher perspective.

People may make plans in their minds,
but the LORD decides what they will do.

PROVERBS 16:9 NCV

Sun-Kissed Souls

In the heavens God has pitched a tent for the sun. ... It rises at one end of the heavens and makes its circuit to the other; nothing is deprived of its warmth.

PSALM 19:4–6 NIV

It looks to be a blustery day today as you head outside, determined for a morning walk. Dressed in gloves and what you thought would be warm pants, you quickly acknowledge the miscalculation. Coldness like liquid seeps through your clothes, chilling your skin, sending shivers all over. Goosebumps spring up on your arms and legs despite your determined pace. Eventually, even your bones revolt as a cold-induced rigor mortis starts to set in. Defeated, you start to turn around when a miracle happens. Like the waters of the Red Sea, overhead clouds blow apart, revealing beautiful blue skies beyond. Better yet, the sun in all its golden glory steps out of hiding and showers your body with unbelievable warmth. The painful chill melts under its glow, and your clothes and skin absorb the welcome warmth. Turning back in the right direction, you resume your pace, grateful for the gift that is God's sun.

Can you imagine what our world would be like without warmth? It's one of those wonders we can't live without yet often overlook in our day-to-day lives. Love functions in a similar way. The pleasure of true fellowship and communion with others fills our hearts with life-giving warmth. But even our earthly relationships are rays of hope sent from above. The true source of love and light and eternal warmth comes from the Author of it all. His presence in and through us brings meaning, hope, and the energy needed to persevere through whatever He lays before us.

This morning, soak in God's presence and love for you. Let it wash you in a warmth that you can share with everyone God brings across your path today.

When we arrived in Jerusalem, the believers welcomed us warmly.

ACTS 21:17 GNT

EXPRESSIONS

The LORD make His face shine on you, and be gracious to you; the LORD lift up His countenance on you, and give you peace.

NUMBERS 6:25–26 NASB

You're already nervous. Though you feel confident about your resume and your ability to do the job, you just didn't have a good feeling about the first round of interviews. You sat up straight and tall, but the interviewer rarely looked up from the paper. When you attempted to answer questions, his arms remained crossed, face flat—stern even. The whole affair seemed so tense you were shocked when they called you back for a second interview. Then the CEO walked in with a strong stride and serious expression. You sensed your doom approaching. But suddenly, a great big smile stretched across his face, and he reached out his hand in greeting. "I know you," he said with a grin, and then explained that he had grown up in the same class as your dad. His tone was casual, his expressions positive, and you could feel the pressure ease. It was okay to be yourself, to communicate clearly and confidently without fear of future rejection.

For some people, approaching God in prayer is like an uncomfortable interview. They picture Him stark and angry, brows furrowed, presence demanding. No wonder they reserve prayer for emergency situations. But God is not that way. He declares every ounce of anger toward sin stopped at the cross of Christ. He knows us, His beloved children. We are not only forgiven but also cherished. God's expression toward us is full of light and love, the depths of who we are always meets with His smile.

When you talk to God this morning, imagine the best expression of joy you've ever seen. Then multiply the effect in your mind, and marvel that God's face shines on you today!

The eyes of the Lord are over the righteous,
and his ears are open unto their prayers.

1 PETER 3:12 KJV

ANCHORS AWAY

Stay grounded and steady in that bond of trust, constantly tuned in to the Message, careful not to be distracted or diverted.

COLOSSIANS 1:22 THE MESSAGE

The skies were the deepest blue, but the crystal clear ocean waters gleamed aquamarine in the warm sunlight. Sitting atop your small boat, you can clearly see the brilliant colors in the coral reef below, the promise of exotic fish and maybe a sea turtle or two tempting you to dive beneath the surface. Slipping into the cool water, you secure your mask and snorkel, ensuring a tight fit. Then you take off, slowly paddling as you float on the surface looking into all the beauty around and below you. Curiosity beckons you forward, but after a while, the thought dawns: *Did I drop anchor?* In a slight panic, you look upward in search of your boat. Finally you see it far in the distance. Switching gears, you swim freestyle and full throttle to the one place you never meant to veer far from.

Experienced snorkelers and scuba divers know the importance of dropping anchor and always staying within sight of the boat. And God's children would do well to apply the same principle in the spiritual realm. The world around us often shines brightly with beautiful attractions. Many of them are given for us to explore, but when we let them lure us away from the foundational truth of God and His Word, we discover danger in what once seemed benign or even beautiful. God repeats the theme throughout His Word: We are to keep our relationship with Him anchored in His Word. Only then can we safely navigate the life-waters of this world.

Where do you stand this morning? Are you anchored securely in God, your relationship rightly tied to His saving grace? Or have you drifted away from center? Without delay, ask God to direct you toward His love and truth this day.

Do not let me wander from Your commandments.
Your word I have treasured in my heart.

PSALM 119:10–11 NASB

BATTLE CRY

*Let petitions and praises shape your worries into prayers,
letting God know your concerns.*

PHILIPPIANS 4:6 THE MESSAGE

Cup of coffee in one hand, plate of buttered toast and egg in the other, you sit down at the table for an early morning breakfast and a quick look at the news. You grab the remote and flip to the channel where you usually find reliable information, only to discover yet another "Breaking News" banner trailing across the screen. As you listen for details behind the latest horrifying story, the spirit inside you recoils at the tragedy. There's so much trouble and heartache in the world, you muse, your sunshine-filled morning now veiled in sadness. With a troubled heart, you press the remote and turn off the TV.

We often feel powerless when we learn of the tremendous pain experienced by people across the world.

But God's people aren't powerless. God has given each of us the most potent weapon in the entire world: prayer. Not the simple, "Saying grace," kind of conversation with God we relegate to meals, but meaty, heartfelt, down-in-the-trenches intercession for our loved ones and all the lost people we've never even met. Down on your knees lifting up other's needs for healing, salvation, and restoration, you access all of heaven's power and pour it out on people and places only God can touch. You are a mighty warrior, valiantly fighting against all the unseen forces of evil in the world, and effecting greater change kneeling beside your couch than you ever could do outside your doors.

This morning, don't despair over evil in the world. Instead, fight with all your energy through the powerful gift of prayer. Our God hears our cry, and He is mighty to save.

I'm standing my ground, GOD, shouting for help, at my prayers every morning, on my knees each daybreak.

PSALM 88:13 THE MESSAGE

Crying may last for a night,
but joy comes in the morning.

PSALM 30:5 NCV

GOLDEN GOODNESS

How sweet your words taste to me; they are sweeter than honey.

PSALM 119:103 NLT

Would you travel 55,000 miles for a pound of honey? Probably not. But a nest of foraging honey bees would put in that kind of work to produce the sweet treat. Each forager bee leaves the hive daily to collect nectar from at least one hundred flowers before returning home. As they suck out the nectar from each flower, they safely store it in a separate stomach—the one reserved just for honey. With their honey tummies full, they fly back to the hive and deposit their golden goodness into hexagonal-shaped honeycomb chambers, capping them with a layer of wax when full. In this way, they have plenty of food stored up for future seasons when winter looms and blooms are scarce. Altogether, it takes more than five hundred bees visiting more than two million flowers to create one pound of honey.

Would you ever have imagined how much work went into that tiny teaspoon of honey you dab on your toast or swirl in your tea? But put it straight on your tongue and you know it's a true golden treasure, the kind of treat only God could mastermind.

It's no wonder, then, that the Psalmist compares God's Word to the sweetness of honey. The Bible you hold in your hands is no ordinary book. It is a miracle of God, the single sweet message of saving grace spoken by God through the pens of ordinary people through the course of more than a thousand years. His labor of love satisfies our souls in a way no other earthly pleasure ever could. This morning, savor the sweetness of God's truth and love, and thank Him for all the extravagant measures He took to bring the truth to your heart.

The laws of the LORD are true; ... They are sweeter than honey,
even honey dripping from the comb.

PSALM 19:9–10 NLT

Jump In

The God of old is your dwelling place, and underneath are the everlasting arms.

DEUTERONOMY 33:27 HCSB

The toddler stood precariously near the edge of the pool, wistfully looking at her father just a few feet away. His arms outstretched, he beckoned his child to jump into his arms. Eyes darted from father to the ever-so-deep water in which he stood. One miscalculation and she might drown, she worried. Growing desperate, she reached out her own arms, leaning forward, hoping he would pick her up off the edge. But it wasn't his plan. Instead, he called her by name. Encouraged her to trust him. And then he patiently waited … until she jumped straight into his arms. Heart beating wildly, the little girl found herself instantly against his chest. The waters around her were indeed deep, but he was taller, stronger. She was safe and warm, right where she wanted to be.

As one observing the situation, it's easy to understand the girl's fears but also the father's heart. Though she felt her world was on the brink of extinction, he knew far better. He was teaching her to trust. And so it is when God calls us to Himself. Though our trials in life seem inevitably devastating, He invites us to trust and jump into His arms. He is not satisfied with simple half-hearted assent or theoretical trust. He wants full heart, mind, and body thrust with complete abandon into His reliable grace and goodness. When we finally leap, we find there is no place better than His warm and certain embrace.

Today, which areas in your life are keeping you sidelined on the edge of full trust? Talk to God in prayer, and take a leap into His loving arms. Discover the place of peace where you've always wanted to be.

You will feel safe because there is hope; you will look around and rest in safety.

JOB 11:18 NCV

MEMORY MARKERS

Don't forget the things you have seen. Don't forget them as long as you live, but teach them to your children and grandchildren.

DEUTERONOMY 4:9 NCV

It's raining outside, and your calendar is clear. Unused to finding empty time on your hands, you are wondering what to do with your day. Then your eyes rest on the bookshelf in the corner, the one where you keep your family's treasures—the trinkets and photos that tell stories of love and laughter throughout the years. *I haven't looked at these albums in ages,* you muse as you wander over and select one from the shelf. Sitting down, you slowly turn the pages and with it the hands of time as your mind remembers the moments. Hours go by. Lost in remembrance, your soul has found shelter in the world of grace in which you and your family have grown.

It's so easy to lose sight of the gifts in the middle of the day's madness, but hindsight paints the picture of purpose

and beauty you couldn't always catch in the moment. God knows our propensity to overlook or even forget His tiny gifts of love tucked into day-to-day busyness. It's why He instructed the people of Israel to set up memorial stones by the Jordan River, so they could remember all the mercies that had led them across. And He loves it when His children do the same, taking time to sit still and reflect on God's amazing faithfulness before the next obligation overtakes them. And be encouraged to record your memories on paper, stones, or whatever helps you keep His hope and grace not on some forgotten bookshelf, but on the forefront of your mind.

This morning, recount His faithfulness and revel in His history of goodness toward you and those you love. Give thanks and celebrate His powerful presence through all the days of your life.

In the future, when your children ask what these stones mean to you, you will tell them. … These stones will always remind the people of Israel of what happened here.

JOSHUA 4:6−7 GNT

ALWAYS HOME

Do you not know that your body is a temple of the Holy Spirit within you, which you have from God, and that you are not your own?

1 CORINTHIANS 6:19 NRSV

Home. It's the one, comfortable place in the whole wide world where you can be the real you. Kick off your shoes and snuggle on the sofa with a really good read. Or rummage through the fridge or pantry to find the food that pleases you most. And while chores might not be the most relaxing or appealing part of home ownership, you don't mind so much because you reap the reward of a well-kept home. You decorate it, maintain it, and appreciate it because it not only tells your story in a unique way, but it's also a place to welcome those you love.

Homes must be special to God, too, because He left heaven to look for one. In the Old Testament, we see that God first walked alongside His people in a beautiful garden.

Longing to be even closer, He instructed His people to build a beautiful tent so He could live right in the middle of them. Wherever they traveled, they took the tent—and God's presence—with them. Later, David and his son Solomon built a glorious temple. But it, too, wasn't quite home enough for God.

When Jesus paid for our sins on the cross, the veil of separation between us and God was torn. And for all who invite Him in, God has come to make His holy home inside our hearts. Whether we're awake or asleep, rejoicing or weeping, questioning or believing, God is at work inside our lives, making Himself a home that reflects His presence.

This morning, thank God that you are a walking, talking miracle of grace as God's presence goes with you in all that you do. Before you, behind you, beside you, and now in you, God has you completely covered by His love.

In him the whole structure is joined together and grows into a holy temple in the Lord.

EPHESIANS 2:21 NRSV

Iron It Out

You have been grieved by various trials, that the genuineness of your faith ... may be found to praise, honor, and glory at the revelation of Jesus Christ,

1 PETER 1:6–7 NKJV

It's amazing what happens when you launder linen. It looks so different than it did when it was hanging so crisp and neat on the store rack. After one washing, that tablecloth has an entirely new texture, and not a desirable one. Millions of mountain ridges have risen over its landscape, and you consider scrapping the entire fabric for something easier to manage. But remembering your budget, you decide to pull out the iron and let it do its magic.

The steam builds. When the temperature is right, you test it to make sure it will have the desired effect. Then you press in, letting the heat and pressure flatten the peaks into a smooth, wide plane, pulling and straightening across the ironing board. Eventually, you realize the restoration process is complete. You have a crisp, clean cover now fit for a king's table.

In a similar way, God has declared us fit for royal dwellings. We have been chosen, forgiven, and loved fully by God. But our lives aren't wrinkle-free yet. Even though we have been laundered by Christ and declared clean in God's sight, we still contend with the wrinkles of a sin nature— that propensity to resist God's ways. But He doesn't toss us out. Instead, He allows the heat and pressure of day-to-day trials to iron out the kinks that keep us from our God-ordained destiny. We are meant for royalty, and He is at work in our lives ironing out the rough edges so we might reflect His glory.

This morning, you may feel the pull and pain of life lived in this world. Don't lose hope. Instead, give thanks that God is at work, turning your life into a beautiful covering for His grace.

Your steadfastness and faith during all your persecutions and
the afflictions … is intended to make you worthy of the kingdom of God.

2 THESSALONIANS 1:4–5 NRSV

PITCHER PERFECT

God has poured out his love to fill our hearts.

ROMANS 5:5 NCV

It was a curious ceramic cylinder sitting in a bucket of water. It seemed to have no purpose at all, no discernable holes or spouts springing from its side. It just boasted one, tall handle that begged lifting. Wondering why anyone would make such an unconventional contraption, you oblige your query by lifting it up and out of the water. And then it starts to pour. Secret holes on the underside allowed the bucket to fill with water until it was full. Now that you are carrying it about, it's emptying itself through those same portholes, watering whatever and wherever you walk with it. Once the water is gone, you simply return it to the bucket, where it fills up once again.

You, child of God, are like that curious watering jar. What you may have felt are weaknesses in your past—painful struggles you'd rather not remember—are the holes in your soul through which God's healing love seeps in. When we sit in His presence, we can't help but soak in His life-giving grace. We were actually designed to hold it inside. But God ordains those portholes for other purposes, too. Not only do life's difficulties draw us closer to Him, but He also intends to use them to bring comfort and nourishment to others in the world.

When God lifts you out of your comfort zone, don't panic or try to plug up the cracks. You were made for this! Instead, let the truth of God's love and grace pour through you into the wilting world around you, knowing that you are being carried in the greatest of hands.

Their buckets will brim with water,
their seed will spread life everywhere.

NUMBERS 24:7 THE MESSAGE

197

GONE FISHING

Jesus called out to them, "Come, follow me! And I will make you fishermen for the souls of men!"

MARK 1:17 TLB

You've always wanted to try it, and now that you're on vacation with your little ones and the weather is right, you decide to give it a go. So you head to the tackle shop with your kids in tow and try to act like you know exactly what you're doing. Unfortunately, you discover an umpteen number of fishing-rod options, along with an entire wall of lures and jigs that all promise success. Of course, there's always the live bait—which seems to be of particular interest to your crew. So you purchase the day's entertainment, praying that at least one person will catch something.

As you stand on the lake's shore, you recognize some potential pitfalls—weeds to the left and low-hanging branches to the right. But everyone is champing at the bit to get their big worms on small hooks. So you get started. Though lines tangle and minnows steal the bait, eventually each kid catches a fish about the size of his or her small hands. You feel grateful for the success and the memories.

Jesus compared faith sharing with fishing. Of course, He was talking to some real-life fishermen who could easily understand the connection, but the analogy isn't lost on us either. Sharing our faith can be daunting, but God tells us not to worry. Witnessing isn't setting a hook. It's sharing your story. The lure to hearers is actually God's Spirit, who brings in the catch when He's ready. We simply make the effort to drop a line by talking to others about what God has done. Today, ask God to help you fish for people. Ask Him to place on your heart those who need to hear His encouraging words and bait your conversation with the beauty of God's love.

Jesus said to them, "Come with me. ... I'll show you how to catch men and women instead of perch and bass."

MATTHEW 4:19 THE MESSAGE

SANDCASTLES

Everyone who hears these words of Mine and acts on them will be like a sensible man who built his house on the rock.

MATTHEW 7:24 HCSB

You're aware of the sun moving toward its peak overhead. There will be no sunburn on your watch. So you pick up the funny castle-shaped bucket and flimsy green plastic spade and get to work helping your kids finish their sandcastle. Before long, though, you feel the sweat coming on—along with your more perfectionistic urges. "We need a deeper moat and higher walls," you hear yourself say. "Keep the turrets nice and trim by adding wetter sand. And how about we find some shells and seaweed for decoration?" It's as if some alien force has put you under its power. *Why on earth am I putting so much effort into something the surf will wash away in minutes?* you wonder.

And then you think again. It's not so different from

real life, really. We often spend all our mental and physical energy trying to build a successful life: the right education with the best grades, the most lucrative career, the best-decorated house, the right car, the most lavish vacations. Yet somewhere in the middle of the madness, we know those investments won't yield the lasting pleasure our hearts long for. And Jesus confirms our suspicions. He likens those pursuits to building castles in the sand. Instead, He instructs us to build our lives on the rock—God Himself. He invites us to put down our plastic shovels and move to the only solid ground that brings true joy and won't be washed away by the rising tide of adversity.

Today, will you settle for building sandcastles, or will you seek firmer ground? Commit your decisions, your dreams, and your heart to the Lord, and let Him show you the best way to build your life in Him.

Store up your treasures in heaven, where moths and rust cannot destroy them, and thieves cannot break in and steal them

MATTHEW 6:20 CEV

IN a NUTSHELL

I pray that Christ Jesus and the church will forever bring praise to God. His power at work in us can do far more than we dare ask or imagine.

EPHESIANS 3:20–21 CEV

To everyone else, it was just a legume, a soil-dweller not destined for anything fancy. Peanuts, after all, had been enjoyed for hundreds of years for what they were. But young George Washington Carver saw something more. It started with just a handful of peanut recipes and uses he discovered when applying his past experience with and knowledge of plants. But soon more ideas sprouted, and the list of applications grew. From one little peanut, Dr. Carver produced more than three hundred highly useful, versatile, and affordable products that helped sustain a strained and struggling farming economy in the South.

Dr. Carver taught a life lesson far greater than even his botanist contributions—recognizing that potential depends on our perspective. Had he acquiesced to culture and even history, he would have never pushed to see just how far that little peanut could go. You, child of God, might feel like life is just too crazy complicated, too overwhelming, or even too boring to bring any change into this world. In a nutshell, you have something in common with those peanuts. But your perspective on this day is the eternal game changer. Are you going to see yourself as only one of six billion people in this world without any real power to contribute something greater? Or will you look at your core component—the God of this universe—who declares you to be of infinite worth? If you dare to believe, you open yourself to all the potential God has packed into the person you are.

Today, let God broaden your perspective of His power working through your unique gifts and abilities. Dare to dream big, and ask Him to multiply His gifts as He pours out His grace through you today.

"If I can?" Jesus asked. "Anything is possible if you have faith."

CURTAIN CALL

O send out Your light and Your truth, let them lead me.

PSALM 43:3 NASB

The room is shrouded in darkness. Furniture silhouettes in varying shades of gray peek out from the shadows beyond your bed, but you are ready to get up and get the day started. You know from your clock the sun must be up, but your blackout drapes are doing their job, and not a peek of light slips past them. So you shuffle over to the wall of curtains on the far side of the room, being careful not to trip on anything along the way and begin pushing apart the panels of fabric. Instantly, light floods the room, shadows vanish, color springs to life, and the beauty that had been in darkness now gleams with fresh vitality.

Our problem is, we often have blackout drapes of a different kind blocking the portals of our souls. When we indulge insecurity, shame, or regret, we find ourselves fumbling around in the shadows. But God who gives us the sun also gives us His Son—the One who radiates light and hope into every corner of our minds and lives. When we risk authentic vulnerability in His presence and allow His Spirit to push back the drapes we have used to hide our unseemly side, His beautiful light rushes in and brings life and color to our souls.

What area of your life needs God's glorious truth and light today? You are always safe in your Father's presence. Present yourself to Him in all honesty this morning and experience the rush of joy and freedom that can only come when you open yourself up fully to God's love.

In Him was life, and the life was the Light of men.

JOHN 1:4 NASB

The Sovereign LORD has given me
his words of wisdom, so that I
know how to comfort the weary.
Morning by morning he wakens me
and opens my understanding to his will.

ISAIAH 50:4 NLT

If I ride the wings of the morning,
  if I dwell by the farthest oceans,
even there your hand will guide me,
and your strength will support me.

PSALM 139:9–10 NLT

Dear Friend,

This book was prayerfully crafted with you, the reader, in mind—every word, every sentence, every page—was thoughtfully written, designed, and packaged to encourage you...right where you are this very moment. At DaySpring, our vision is to see every person experience the life-changing message of God's love. So, as we worked through rough drafts, design changes, edits and details, we prayed for you to deeply experience His unfailing love, indescribable peace, and pure joy. It is our sincere hope that through these Truth-filled pages your heart will be blessed, knowing that God cares about you—your desires and disappointments, your challenges and dreams.

He knows. He cares. He loves you unconditionally.

BLESSINGS!
THE DAYSPRING BOOK TEAM

**Additional copies of this book and
other DaySpring titles can be purchased
at fine bookstores everywhere.
Order online at dayspring.com
or
by phone at 1-877-751-4347**